P9-EMQ-056

C·R·A·Z·Y ENGLISH

The Ultimate Joy Ride
Through
Our Language

Books by Richard Lederer

Crazy English
Get Thee to a Punnery
Anguished English

C·R·A·Z·Y ENGLISH

The Ultimate Joy Ride Through Our Language

RICHARD LEDERER

POCKET BOOKS
New York London Toronto Sydney Tokyo

Versions of many of the chapters in this book have appeared in *Verbatim, Writing!,* and *Word Ways.*

Another *Original* publication of POCKET BOOKS

POCKET BOOKS, a division of Simon & Schuster Inc.
1230 Avenue of the Americas, New York, NY 10020

ISBN: 0-671-68906-1

First Pocket Books hardcover printing September 1989

10 9 8 7 6 5 4 3 2 1

Printed in the U.S.A.

To my family, for always encouraging me
to build castles in the air;

To Pete and Robin, for putting
the foundations underneath;

To Stacy, for her lovely interior decorating.

Contents

I

The Strange Case of the English Language

"Like the fabled Jabberwock, words have jaws that bite and claws that catch."

—JAMES J. KILPATRICK

English Is a Crazy Language

English is the most widely spoken language in the history of our planet, used in some way by at least one out of every seven human beings around the globe. Half of the world's books are written in English, and the majority of international telephone calls are made in English. English is the language of over sixty percent of the world's radio programs, many of them beamed, ironically, by the Russians, who know that to win friends and influence nations, they're best off using English. More than seventy percent of international mail is written and addressed in English, and eighty percent of all computer text is stored in English. English has acquired the largest vocabulary of all the world's languages, perhaps as many as two million words, and has generated one of the noblest bodies of literature in the annals of the human race.

Nonetheless, it is now time to face the fact that English is a crazy language.

In the crazy English language, the blackbird hen is brown, blackboards can be blue or green, and blackberries are green and then red before they are ripe. Even if blackberries were really black and blueberries really blue, what are strawberries, cranberries, elderberries, huckleberries, raspberries, boysenberries, and gooseberries supposed to look like?

To add to the insanity, there is no butter in buttermilk, no egg in eggplant, neither worms nor wood in wormwood, neither pine nor apple in pineapple, and no ham in a hamburger. (In fact, if somebody invented a sandwich consisting of a ham patty in a bun, we would have a hard time finding a name for it.) To make matters worse, English muffins weren't invented in England, french fries in France, or Danish pastries in Denmark. And we discover even more culinary madness in the revelations that sweetmeat is made from fruit, while sweetbread, which isn't sweet, is made from meat.

In this unreliable English tongue, greyhounds aren't always grey (or gray), ladybugs and fireflies are beetles, a panda bear is a raccoon, a koala bear is a marsupial, a guinea pig is neither a pig nor from Guinea, and a titmouse is neither mammal nor mammaried.

Language is like the air we breathe. It's invisible, inescapable, indispensable, and we take it for granted. But when we take the time to explore the paradoxes and vagaries of English, we find that hot dogs can be cold, darkrooms can be lit, homework can be done in school, nightmares can take place in broad daylight while morning sickness and daydreaming can take place at night, midwives can be men, hours—especially happy hours and rush hours—can last longer than sixty minutes, quicksand works *very* slowly, boxing rings are square, silverware can be made of plastic and tablecloths of paper, most telephones are dialed by being punched (or pushed?), and most bathrooms don't have any baths in them. In fact, a dog can go to the bathroom under a tree—no bath, no room; it's still going to the bathroom. And doesn't it seem at least a little bizarre that we go to the bathroom in order to go to the bathroom?

Why is it that a woman can man a station but a man can't woman one, that a man can father a movement but a woman can't mother one, and that a king rules a kingdom but a queen doesn't rule a queendom? How did all those Renaissance men reproduce when there doesn't seem to have been any Renaissance women?

A writer is someone who writes, and a stinger is something that stings. But fingers don't fing, grocers don't groce, hammers don't ham, and humdingers don't hum. If the plural of *tooth* is *teeth*, shouldn't the plural of *booth* be *beeth*? One goose, two geese—so one moose, two meese? One index, two indices—one Kleenex, two Kleenices? If people ring a bell today and rang a bell yesterday, why don't we say that they flang a ball? If they wrote a letter, perhaps they also bote their tongue. If the teacher taught, why isn't it also true that the preacher praught? Why is it that the sun shone yesterday while I shined my shoes, that I treaded water and then trod on soil, and that I flew out to see a World Series game in which my favorite player flied out?

If we conceive a conception and receive at a reception, why don't we grieve a greption and believe a beleption? If

HEAD OVER HEELS
IN LOVE
WATCH
YOUR HEAD
BACKWARD

a horsehair mat is made from the hair of horses and a camel's hair brush from the hair of camels, from what is a mohair coat made? If a vegetarian eats vegetables, what does a humanitarian eat? If a firefighter fights fire, what does a freedom fighter fight? If a weightlifter lifts weights, what does a shoplifter lift? If *pro* and *con* are opposites, is congress the opposite of progress?

Sometimes you have to believe that all English speakers should be committed to an asylum for the verbally insane. In what other language do people drive in a parkway and park in a driveway? In what other language do people recite at a play and play at a recital? In what other language do privates eat in the general mess and generals eat in the private mess? In what other language do people ship by truck and send cargo by ship? In what other language can your nose run and your feet smell?

How can a slim chance and a fat chance be the same and a bad licking and a good licking be the same, while a wise man and a wise guy are opposites? How can sharp speech and blunt speech be the same and *quite a lot* and *quite a few* the same, while *overlook* and *oversee* are opposites? How can the weather be hot as hell one day and cold as hell the next?

If *button* and *unbutton* and *tie* and *untie* are opposites, why are *loosen* and *unloosen* and *ravel* and *unravel* the same? If *bad* is the opposite of *good*, *hard* the opposite of *soft*, and *up* the opposite of *down*, why are *badly* and *goodly*, *hardly* and *softly*, and *upright* and *downright* not opposing pairs? If harmless actions are the opposite of harmful actions, why are shameless and shameful behavior the same and pricey objects less expensive than priceless ones? If appropriate and inappropriate remarks and passable and impassable mountain trails are opposites, why are flammable and inflammable materials, heritable and inheritable property, and passive and impassive people the same and valuable objects less treasured than invaluable ones? If *uplift* is the same as *lift up*, why are *upset* and *set up* opposite in meaning? Why are *pertinent* and *impertinent, canny* and *uncanny,* and *famous* and *infamous* neither opposites nor the same? How can *raise* and *raze* and *reckless* and *wreckless* be opposites when each pair contains the same sound?

Why is it that when the sun or the moon or the stars are out, they are visible, but when the lights are out, they are invisible, and that when I wind up my watch, I start it, but when I wind up this essay, I shall end it?

English is a crazy language.

How can expressions like "I'm mad about my flat," "No football coaches allowed," and "I'll come by in the morning and knock you up" convey such different messages in two countries that purport to speak English?

How can it be easier to assent than to dissent but harder to ascend than to descend? Why is it that a man with hair on his head has more hair than a man with hairs on his head; that if you decide to be bad forever, you choose to be bad for good; and that if you choose to wear only your left shoe, then your left one is right and your right one is left? Right?

Small wonder that we English users are constantly standing meaning on its head. Let's look at a number of familiar English words and phrases that turn out to mean the opposite of or something very different from what we think they mean:

I could care less. *I couldn't care less* is the clearer, more accurate version. Why do so many people delete the negative from this statement? Because they are afraid that the *n't . . . less* combination will make for a double negative, which is a no-no.

I really miss not seeing you. Whenever people say this to me, I feel like saying, "All right, I'll leave!" Here speakers throw in a gratuitous negative, *not*, even though *I really miss seeing you* is what they want to say.

The movie kept me literally glued to my seat. The chances of our buttocks being literally epoxied to a seat are about as small as the chances of our literally rolling in the aisles while watching a funny movie or literally drowning in tears while watching a sad one. We actually mean *The movie kept me figuratively glued to my seat*—but who needs *figuratively*, anyway? If we must resort to a cliché, *The movie kept me glued to my seat* is the clearest, most sensible way of expressing our emotions.

Put your best foot forward. Now, let's see . . . We have a good foot, a better foot, but we don't have a third—and best—foot. It's our better foot that we want to put forward. "Put your best foot forward" is akin to "May the best team win." Usually there are only two teams in the contest.

A near miss. *A near miss* is, in reality, a collision. A close call is actually *a near hit*.

My idea fell between the cracks. If something *fell between the cracks*, didn't it land smack on the planks or the concrete? Shouldn't that be *My idea fell into the cracks*?

I'll follow you to the ends of the earth. Let the

word go forth to the four corners of the Earth that ever since Columbus we have known that the earth doesn't have any ends.

A hot cup of coffee. Who cares if the cup is hot? Surely we mean *a cup of hot coffee*.

A one-night stand. So who's standing?

Doughnut holes. Aren't these little treats really *doughnut balls*? The holes are what's left in the original doughnut. (And if a candy cane is shaped like a cane, why isn't a doughnut shaped like a nut?)

I want to have my cake and eat it too. Shouldn't this timeworn cliché be *I want to eat my cake and have it too*? Isn't the logical sequence that one hopes to eat the cake and then still possess it?

The announcement was made by a nameless official. Just about everybody has a name, even officials. Surely what is meant is *The announcement was made by an unnamed official*.

Preplan, preboard, and preheat. Aren't people who do this simply planning, boarding, and heating? Who needs the pre-tentious prefix?

Put on your shoes and socks. This is an exceedingly difficult maneuver. Most of us put on our socks first, then our shoes.

The bus goes back and forth between the terminal and the airport. Again we find mass confusion about the order of events. You have to go forth before you can go back.

Underwater and **underground.** Things that we claim are *underwater* and *underground* are obviously surrounded by, not under, the water and ground.

I got caught in one of the biggest traffic bottle-

one of the biggest traffic bottlenecks

necks of the year. The bigger the bottleneck, the more freely the contents of the bottle flow through it. To be true to the metaphor, we should say, *I got caught in one of the smallest bottlenecks of the year*.

I lucked out. To *luck out* sounds as if you're out of luck. Don't you mean, *I lucked in?*

Because we speakers and writers of English seem to have our heads screwed on backward, we constantly misperceive our bodies, often saying just the opposite of what we mean:

Watch your head. I keep seeing this sign on low doorways, but I haven't figured out how to follow the instructions. Trying to watch your head is like trying to bite your teeth.

They're head over heels in love. That's nice, but all of us do almost everything *head over heels*. If we are trying to create an image of people doing cartwheels and somersaults, why don't we say, *They're heels over head in love*?

Keep a stiff upper lip. When we are disappointed or afraid, which lip do we try to control? The lower lip, of course, is the one we are trying to keep from quivering.

I'm speaking tongue in cheek. So how can anyone understand you?

They do things behind my back. You want they should do things in front of your back?

They did it ass backwards. What's wrong with that? How else are they supposed to do it?

English is weird.

In the rigid expressions that wear tonal grooves in the record of our language, *beck* can appear only with *call*, *cranny* with *nook*, *hue* with *cry*, *main* with *might*, *fettle* only with *fine*, *aback* with *taken*, *caboodle* with *kit*, and *spic* and *span* only with each other. Why must all shrifts be short, all lucre filthy, all bystanders innocent, and all bedfellows strange? I'm convinced that some shrifts are lengthy and that some lucre is squeaky clean, and I've certainly met guilty bystanders and perfectly normal bedfellows.

Why is it that only swoops are fell? Sure, the verbivorous William Shakespeare invented the expression "one fell swoop," but why can't strokes, swings, acts, and the like also be fell? Why are we allowed to vent our spleens but never our kidneys or livers? Why must it be only our minds that are boggled, and never our eyes or our hearts? Why can't eyes and jars be ajar, as well as doors? Why must aspersions always be cast and never hurled or lobbed?

Doesn't it seem just a little loopy that we can make amends but never just one amend; that no matter how carefully we comb through the annals of history, we can never discover just one annal; that we can never pull a shenanigan, be in a doldrum, or get a jitter, a willy, a delirium tremen, or a heebie-jeebie; and that, sifting through the wreckage of a disaster, we can never find just one smithereen? Indeed, this whole business of plurals that don't have matching singulars reminds me to ask this burning linguistic question, one that has puzzled scholars for decades: If you have a bunch of odds and ends and you get rid of or sell off all but one of them, what do you call that doohickey with which you're left?

What do you make of the fact that we can talk about certain things and ideas only when they are absent? Once they appear, our blessed English doesn't allow us to describe them. Have you ever seen a horseful carriage or a strapful gown? Have you ever run into someone who was combobulated, sheveled, gruntled, chalant, plussed, ruly, gainly, maculate, pecunious, or peccable? Have you ever met a sung hero or experienced requited love? I know people who are no spring chickens, but where, pray tell, are the people who *are* spring chickens? Where are the people who actually *would* hurt a fly? All the time I meet people who *are* great shakes, who *can* cut the mustard, who *can* fight City Hall, who *are* my cup of tea, and whom I *would* touch with a ten-foot pole, but I cannot talk about them in English.

If the truth be told, all languages are a little crazy. As Walt Whitman might proclaim, they contradict themselves. That's because language is invented, not discovered, by boys and girls and men and women, not computers. As such, language reflects the creativity and fearful asymmetry of the human race, which, of course, isn't really a race at all. That's why *six, seven, eight*, and *nine* change to *sixty, seventy, eighty*, and *ninety*, but *two, three, four*, and *five* do not become *twoty, threety, fourty*, and *fivety*. That's why we can turn lights off and on but not out and in. That's why we wear a pair of pants but, except on very cold days, never a pair of shirts. That's why we can open up the floor, climb the walls, raise the roof, pick up the house, and bring down the house.

In his essay "The Awful German Language," Mark Twain spoofs the confusion engendered by German gender by translating literally from a conversation in a German Sunday school book: "*Gretchen*. Wilhelm, where is the turnip? *Wilhelm*. She has gone to the kitchen. *Gretchen*. Where is the accomplished and beautiful English maiden?

Wilhelm. It has gone to the opera." Twain continues: "A tree is male, its buds are female, its leaves are neuter; horses are sexless, dogs are male, cats are female—tomcats included."

Still, you have to marvel at the unique lunacy of the English language, in which your house can simultaneously burn up and burn down, in which you fill in a form by filling out a form, in which you add up a column of figures by adding them down, in which your alarm clock goes off by going on, in which you are inoculated for measles by being inoculated against measles, and in which you first chop a tree down—and then you chop it up.

Confusable English

I once attended a series of seminars that explored the realities of living in a nuclear age. The last of these programs included a debate about the Strategic Defense Initiative, popularly known as Star Wars, between a naval commander representing the Defense Department and a university physics professor. As one would guess, the commander stoutly defended Star Wars as being both scientifically feasible and strategically desirable. As his speech soared to its conclusion the Pentagonian exulted, "In Star Wars, America has finally come up with the penultimate defense system!"

Oops. Do you grasp the gaffe, follow the faux pas, make out the malapropism, and spot the solecism in the Commander's use of the word *penultimate*? The speaker obviously thought that *penultimate* means "the absolute ultimate." So do a lot of us, including the Tony Award winner who gushed, "I knew what my goal was when I saw Lauren Bacall touring in a play in Buffalo. To be an actress like that—well, to me that was the penultimate!"

But *penultimate* doesn't mean the absolute ultimate. (Can anything be more than ultimate?) Derived from the Latin *paene*, "almost," and *ultimus*, "last," *penultimate* means "next to last." Thinking that *pen-* was an intensifier rather than a qualifier, our naval commander ended up saying the opposite of what he meant. The last thing we want is a penultimate defense system against nuclear weapons.

Now have a look at this message: "The Bureau of Animal Affairs will help you get those clucking, flapping pigeons off your window ledge, and will issue a summons to those who scatter food that attracts bands of the noisome birds." Oops again. The Bureau writer, like many other English users, apparently thought that *noisome* means "noisy." But *noisome* has nothing to do with noise. In truth, the word is formed from a shortening of *annoy* plus the adjectival suffix *-some*. Most frequently, *noisome* is used to describe an offensive odor, annoying to the point of being nauseating.

Similar to *noisome* is *fulsome*. A general was in the habit of extending his "most fulsome congratulations" to medal recipients. It is true that the original meaning of *fulsome* was "full, abundant," but the well-meaning general overlooked the dominant sense of the word today, "offensive to the senses or sensibility," and damned with misguided praise.

"O Romeo,
Romeo! wherefore
art thou Romeo?"

Then there's the catalog of high school English books with a cartoon on the cover showing William Shakespeare's Juliet standing on her balcony, gazing off into the distance, and asking, "Wherefore art thou, teaching aids?" Lower on the page, Romeo stares up at Juliet and says, "Inside! Eighteen new publications plus many other fine materials." I would hope that most of my fellow inmates in the house of correction (of composition) caught the blooper. Quite obviously, the publisher of English materials interpreted *wherefore* as meaning "where," a mistake that has been perpetrated and perpetuated by generations of would-be Shakespearean actresses who misconstrue the famous line in *Romeo and Juliet*, "O Romeo, Romeo! wherefore art thou Romeo?" But a knowledgeable examination of Shakespeare's language—"Wherefore rejoice?/ What conquest brings he home?" (*Julius Caesar*); "But wherefore could I not pronounce 'Amen'?" (*Macbeth*)—reveals that *wherefore* means "why," not "where," further proof being the redundant cliché "the whys and wherefores." Thus, those who deliver the sentence "Wherefore art thou Romeo?" should place emphasis on the word *Romeo* rather than on the word *art*. And any teaching aid that advertises itself by questioning its own existence is falling down in the marketing department.

"Bird had staggered into the All-Star Game with back-to-back stinkeroos against Indiana (7 for 19) and Milwaukee (7-24). But winning the Three-Point title always enervates him, even as taking it relatively easy for three days refreshes him," reads a news story on Celtics star forward Larry Bird. From the context of the article we can be certain that the writer succumbed to another common foot-in-mouth error and thought that *enervate* means "to energize," when it really means "to weaken."

Penultimate, *noisome*, *fulsome*, *wherefore*, and *enervate* are five especially deceptive, noisome, and fulsome words in sheep's clothing, words that don't mean what they look like they should mean. Here is a small quiz that presents more words that are not what they seem. Beware and be wary as you choose the correct definition for each entry. Avoid taking a simplistic (there's another one!) approach. Answers repose at the end of this book.

1. *antebellum* *a*. against women *b*. against war *c*. after the war *d*. before the war

2. *apiary* *a*. school for mimics *b*. place where apes are kept *c*. place where bees are kept *d*. cupboard for peas

3. *aquiline* *a*. resembling an eagle *b*. relating to water *c*. relating to synchronized swimming *d*. resembling a porcupine

4. *cupidity* *a*. strong desire for wealth *b*. strong desire for love *c*. strong desire for amusement parks *d*. obtuseness

5. *disinterested* *a*. lacking a bank account *b*. unbiased *c*. bored *d*. lacking rest

6. *enormity* *a*. great wickedness *b*. great size *c*. normal state *d*. cowardice

7. *forestress* *a*. ancient hair style *b*. female forester *c*. dread anticipation *d*. emphasis on first part of word

8. *friable* *a*. easily crumbled *b*. easily fried *c*. unhealthy *d*. relating to holy orders

9. *herpetology* the study of *a*. herbs *b*. herpes *c*. female pets *d*. reptiles

10. *hippophobia* the fear of *a*. hippopotami *b*. horses *c*. getting fat *d*. hippies

11. *infinitesimal* *a*. very small *b*. very large *c*. relating to intestines *d*. hesitant

12. *inflammable* *a*. calm *b*. incredulous *c*. not easily set on fire *d*. easily set on fire

13. *ingenuous* *a*. insincere *b*. innocent *c*. clever *d*. mentally dull

14. *meretricious* *a*. falsely attractive *b*. worthy *c*. good tasting *d*. diseased

15. *presently* *a*. generous with gifts *b*. now *c*. soon *d*. presidentially

16. *prosody* the study of *a*. drama *b*. music *c*. prose *d*. versification

17. *restive* *a*. serene *b*. festive *c*. fidgety *d*. pensive

18. *risible* *a.* disposed to laugh *b.* easily lifted *c.* fertile *d.* relating to dawn

19. *toothsome* *a.* displaying prominent teeth *b.* missing teeth *c.* palatable *d.* serrated

20. *votary* *a.* democratic country *b.* enthusiast *c.* electoral college *d.* revolving tool

Good Grief!

Not long ago, a couple that I know tooled down to a local car emporium to look over the latest products. Attracted to the low sticker price on the basic model, they told the salesman that they were considering buying an unadorned automobile and had no inclination to purchase any of the long list of options affixed to the side window of the vehicle they were inspecting.

"But you will have to pay $168 for the rear window wiper," the salesman explained.

"But we don't want the rear wiper," my friends protested.

And the salesman said: "We want to keep the sticker price low, but every car comes with the rear window wiper. So you have to buy it. It's a mandatory option."

Mandatory option is a telling example of the kind of

Good grief! What's an oxymoron?

pushme-pullyou doublespeak that pervades the language of business and politics these days. It is also a striking instance of an oxymoron.

"Good grief!" you exclaim. "What's an oxymoron?"

An oxymoron (I reply) is a figure of speech in which two incongruous, contradictory terms are yoked together in a small space. As a matter of fact, *good grief* is an oxymoron.

Appropriately, the word *oxymoron* is itself oxymoronic because it is formed from two Greek roots of opposite meaning—*oxys*, "sharp, keen," and *moros*, "foolish," the same root that gives us the word *moron*. Two other examples of foreign word parts oxymoronically drawn to each other are *pianoforte*, "soft-loud," and *sophomore*, "wise fool." If you know any sophomoric sophomores, you know how apt that oxymoron is.

I have long been amused by the name of a grocery store in my town, West Street Superette, since *super* means "large" and *-ette* means "small." If you have a superette in your town, it is a "large small" store.

Perhaps the best known oxymoron in the United States is one from comedian George Carlin's record *Toledo Window Box*, the delightful *jumbo shrimp*. Expand the expression to *fresh frozen jumbo shrimp*, and you have a double oxymoron. In a dazzling and dazing triple oxymoron, another comedian, Jay Leno, was recently named a "permanent guest host" for the "Tonight" show.

Once you start collecting oxymora (just as the plural of *phenomenon* is *phenomena*, an oxymoron quickly becomes a list of oxymora), these compact two-word paradoxes start popping up everywhere you look. Among the prize specimens in my trophy case are these *minor mira-*

cles, and I hope that they will go over better than a *lead balloon:*

old news
even odds
flat busted
pretty ugly
civil war
awful good
inside out
spendthrift
small fortune
a dull roar
growing small
same difference
dry ice (or beer)
white chocolate (or gold)
industrial park
half naked
open secret
sight unseen
baby grand
loyal opposition
working vacation
idiot savant
loose tights
student teacher
light heavyweight
original copy
recorded live
standard deviation
freezer burn
divorce court
criminal justice
cardinal sin
death benefit
conspicuously absent
constructive criticism
negative growth
build down
elevated subway
mobile home
benign neglect
plastic silverware
deliberate speed
living end
random order
flexible freeze
benevolent despot
tight slacks

Literary oxymora, created *accidentally on purpose*, include Geoffrey Chaucer's *hateful good*, Edmund Spenser's *proud humility*, John Milton's *darkness visible*, Alexander Pope's "damn with *faint praise,*" James Thomson's

mobile home

"*expressive silence,*" Lord Byron's *melancholy merriment*, Alfred, Lord Tennyson's *falsely true*, Ernest Hemingway's *scalding coolness*, and, the most quoted of all, William Shakespeare's "parting is such *sweet sorrow.*" Abraham Lincoln's political opponent, Stephen Douglas, was known as the *Little Giant*, and, more recently, Dallas Cowboys football coach Tom Landry commented before a Super Bowl that he was feeling *confidently scared*.

Now, if you are willing to stretch the oxymoronic concept and editorialize unabashedly, you will expand your oxymoronic list considerably. Thus, we can observe natural oxymora, literary oxymora, and opinion oxymora, three categories that are not always *mutually exclusive*:

nonworking mother
military intelligence
young Republican
peace offensive
Peacekeeper Missile
war games
business ethics
United Nations
student athlete
safe sex
educational television
rock music
civil engineer
designer jeans
postal service
Amtrak schedule
Greater (your choice of scapegoat city)
President (your choice of scapegoat president)
Iranian moderate
Moral Majority

Oxymora lurk even in place names, like *Little Big Horn*, *Old New York*, and *Fork Union*, and in single words, like *bittersweet*, *firewater*, *preposterous*, *semiboneless*, *wholesome*, and *Noyes*. If you have trouble understanding that last one, examine its first two and then its last three letters.

Good grief! Oxymora are everywhere!

Sesquipedalian English

Early in my career as a verbivore, I became fascinated with long words. I was delighted when I happened upon *inappropriateness* (seventeen letters) and *incomprehensibility* (nineteen letters), and then I was introduced to the twenty-eight-letter *antidisestablishmentarianism.* Because that word is the most famous of all polysyllabic creations, it is worth dissecting in some detail: *anti-* "against," *dis-* "reversal," *establish* (the root of the word) "to secure," *ment-* "result or agent of an action," *arian-* "believing," and *ism-* "doctrine." Stitching together these pieces, we find that *antidisestablishmentarianism* means "a doctrine against the dissolution of the establishment." In the nineteenth century, the word meant "opposition to the separation of the established church and state."

Only in my early middle age did I discover that *anti-*

a mere pygmy

disestablishmentarianism is a mere pygmy in the hierarchy of truly long words. Here is a sampler of giant words, each of which reposes in at least one reputable dictionary. Gazing upon their length and bulk reminds us of the bizarre shapes that English words can assume.

floccinaucinihilipilification (twenty-nine letters): the categorizing of something as worthless or trivial. The word dates back to 1741 and is the longest word in the *Oxford English Dictionary.* In it the letter *i* occurs nine times and the letter *e* not at all.

hippopotomonstrosesquipedalian (thirty letters): pertaining to a very long word. How appropriate.

supercalifragilisticexpialidocious (thirty-four letters): a word invented for the film *Mary Poppins* (1964) that has become the best known word of more than twenty-eight letters. Etymologically this is not entirely a nonsense word: *super-* "above," *cali-* "beauty," *fragilistic-* "delicate," *expiali-* "to atone," and *docious-* "educable," the sum of which equals "atoning for extreme and delicate beauty [while being] highly educable."

pneumonoultramicroscopicsilicovolcanoconiosis (forty-five letters): a miners' lung disease caused by the inhalation of silicate or quartz dust. This longest of all words entered in *Webster's Third New International Dictionary* can be broken down into *pneumono-* "lung," *ultra-* "beyond," *micro-* "small," *scopic-* "to see," *silico-* "flint, quartz," *volcano-* "fiery, as from a volcano," *keni-* "dust," and *osis-* "a diseased condition," yielding "a disease of the lungs [caused by] dust from volcanic ash [so fine as to be] beyond the range of [an instrument that] sees very small [things]."

Such hippopotomonstrosesquipedalian entries have inspired me to create a polysyllabic limerick:

> It's true that I have halitosis.
> At least it's not
> pneumonoultramicroscopicsilicovolcanoconiosis.
>   Thus, rather than floccinaucinihilipilification,
>   I feel only elation
> That's supercalifragilisticexpialidocious.

Moving beyond *pneumonoultramicroscopicsilicovolcanoconiosis*, we come to *Chargoggagoggmanchaug gagoggchaubunagungamaugg* (forty-five letters, fifteen of them *g*'s): a Native American name for a lake near Webster, Massachusetts. The name means "You fish on your side; I fish on my side; nobody fish in the middle."

Taumatawhakata . . . : So begins the unofficial eighty-five-letter version of the name of a hill in New Zealand, believed to be the longest place name in the world. The name means "the place where Tametea, the man with the big knee who slid, climbed, and swallowed mountains, known as Land-eater, played the flute to his loved one."

bothallchoractora . . . : the beginning of one of ten "thunderwords" in James Joyce's *Finnegans Wake,* each of which is made up of a hundred letters.

acetylseryltyrosyl . . . : These are the first of 1,185 letters that make up the protein part of the tobacco mosaic virus. Fortunately, the molecule can be reduced to the formula C785H122ON2120248S2.

But not done. For there is one more chemical compound whose name exceeds even the length of the above tobacco chain. Tryptophan synthetase A protein is an enzyme with 267 amino acids. When spelled in full, the

word stretches to 1,913 letters: *methionylglutaminylarginyl-
tyrosylglutamylserylleucylphenylalanylalanylglutaminyl-
leucyllysylglutamylarginyllysylglutamylglycylalanylphenyl-
alanylvalylprolylphenylalanylyalylthreonylleucylglycylas-
partylprolylglycylisoleucylglutamylglutaminylserylleucyl-
lysylisoleucylaspartylthreonylleucylisoleucylglutamylala-
nylglycylalanylaspartylalanylleucylglutamylleucylglycy-
lisoleucylprolylphenylalanylserylaspartylprolylleucelala-
nylaspartylglycylprolylthreonylisoleucylglutaminylaspara-
ginylalanylthreonylleucylarginylalanylphenylalanylalanyl-
alanylglycylvalylthreonylprolylalanylglutaminylcysteinyl-
phenylalanylglutamylmethionylleucyalanylleucylisoleucyl-
arginylglutaminyllysylhistidylprolylthreonylisoleucylpro-
lylisoleucylglycylleucylleucylmethionyltyrosylalanylaspa-
raginylleucylvalylphenylalanylasparaginyllysylglycyliso-
leucylaspartylglutamylphenylalanyltyrosylalanylglutami-
nylcysteinylglutamyllysylvalylglycylvalylaspartylserylva-
lylleucylvalylalanylaspartylvalylprolylvalylglutaminyl-
glutamylserylalanylprolylphenylalanylarginylglutaminyl-
alanylalanylleucylarginylhistidylasparaginylvalylalanyl-
prolylisoleucylphenylalanylisoleucylcysteinylprolylpro-
lylaspartylalanylaspartylaspartylaspartylleucylleucylar-
ginylglutaminylisoleucylalanylseryltyrosylglycylarginyl-
glcyltyrosylthreonyltyrosylleucylleucylserylarginylalanyl-
glycylvalylthreonylglycylalanylglutamylasparaginylar-
ginylanylalanylleucylprolylleucylasparaginylhistidylleu-
cylvalylalanyllysylleucyllysylglutamyltyrosylasparagi-
nylalanylalanylprolylprolylleucylglutaminylglycylphenyl-
alanylglycylisoleucylserylalanylprolylaspartylgluta-
minylvalyllysylalanylalanylisoleucylaspartylalanylglycyl-
alanylalanylglycylalanylisoleucylserylglycylserylala-
nylisoleucylbalyllysylisoleucylisoleucylglutamylgluta-*

minylhistidylasparaginylisoleucylglutamylprolylglutamyllysylmethionylleucylalanylalanylleucyllysylvalylphenylalanylvalylglutaminylprolylmethionyllysylalanylalanylthreonylarginylserine.

So what *is* the longest word in the English language? A children's riddle says *smiles* because there is a "mile" between its first and last letters. But it is comedian Red Skelton who deserves credit for identifying the longest word of all. Skelton maintained that the longest word in the English language is the word that follows the voice that comes on your radio or television set and intones: "And now a word from our sponsors."

II

The Name Is the Game

"To-day we have the naming of the parts."

—Henry Reed

What's Your Phobia?

According to the Mayan sacred book *Popol Vuh*, after the Creators had made the earth, carved it with mountains, valleys, and rivers, and covered it with vegetation, they formed the animals who would be guardians of the plant world and who would praise the Makers' names: " 'Speak, then, our names, praise us, your mother, your father. Invoke, then, Huracan, Chipi-Caculha, the Heart of Heaven, the Heart of Earth, the Creator, the Maker, the Forefathers. Speak, invoke us, adore us.'

"But the animals only hissed and screamed and cackled. They were unable to make words, and each screamed in a different way.

"When the Creator and the Maker saw that it was impossible for them to talk to each other, they said: 'It is

The animals only hissed and screamed and cackled.

impossible for them to say the names of us, their Creators and Makers. This is not well.'

"As a punishment, the birds and animals were condemned to be eaten and sacrificed by others, and the Creators set out to make another creature who would be able to call their names and speak their praises. This creature was man and woman."

In biblical Genesis, we read that God said, "Let us make man in our image, after our likeness," and, as in the Mayan myth of creation, God bestowed upon human beings the power of language, the power to name things: "And out of the ground the Lord God formed every beast of the field, and every fowl of the air; and brought them unto Adam to see what he would call them: and whatsoever Adam called every living creature, that was the name thereof. And Adam gave names to all cattle, and to the fowl of the air, and to every beast of the field."

The human desire and power to name everything is nowhere better demonstrated than in our ability to label our deepest fears—our phobias.

Do you have an undomesticated pet phobia? No? Think again. Does your stomach want to scream when it and you arrive at the zenith of a ferris wheel? Does your head retract turtlelike into your body when the lightning flashes and the thunder cracks? Do you tremble at the sight of a snake or a spider, or a cat and a dog?

Such fears are called phobias. If you are afflicted with a few of these reactions, don't worry; studies show that the average person possesses three phobias. Things could be worse: Count your blessings that you are not a victim of *pantophobia*—the morbid dread of everything. Then you would be stuck with *verbaphobia*, and you wouldn't be able to enjoy this book.

Humankind is beset with a host of fears and has managed to name practically every one of them. Phobos, "fear," was the son of Ares, the god of war, and was the nephew of Eris, goddess of discord, and brother to Deimos, "terror." The names of our deepest dreads generally include the Greek root *phobia*, meaning "fear or hatred," affixed to another root, which is also usually Greek. The two most common human phobias are *acrophobia*, a morbid fear of heights, and *claustrophobia*, a morbid fear of enclosed spaces. Look for your deepest dreads among the lists that follow. By assigning names to these terrors, you may be taking the first step in overcoming them.

Let's start with the creatures with whom we share this planet. From time immemorial, some of these organisms have inspired fear and even terror in the human breast. Each of these dreads has a label: Fear of animals is called *zoophobia*, of birds *ornithophobia*, of fish *ichthyophobia*, of reptiles *herpetophobia*, and of insects *entophobia*.

Here are the names we have contrived for the fears of more specific organisms. In each case, I leave it to you to supply the words "fear of": *acarophobia*: mites, parasites; *aelurophobia*: cats; *apiophobia*: bees; *arachnephobia*: spiders; *bacilliphobia*: bacilli; *bacteriaphobia*: bacteria; *batarachophobia*: frogs, toads; *cynophobia*: termites; *eisoptrophobia*: termites; *entonophobia*: ticks; *galeophobia*: sharks; *hippophobia*: horses; *musophobia*: mice; *myrmecophobia*: lice; *soleciphobia*: worms; *swinophobia*: swine; *taeniophobia*: tapeworms; *taurophobia*: bulls.

We have fewer words to express our fears of flora; evidently, plants are regarded as more docile and less threatening than other organisms: *anthophobia*: flowers, plants; *dendrophobia*: trees; *hylophobia*: forests, woods; *lachanophobia*: vegetables. Hence, if you despise eating spinach or broccoli, *you are a lachanophobe*.

For some of us, it is other people who inspire in our hearts the greatest palpitations—*anthropophobia*. If you fear men, you are afflicted with *androphobia*, if you fear women, *gynephobia*. If it is your relatives who won't get off your nerves, you have *syngenescophobia*. More specifically, if you are irritated by your mother-in-law, you are burdened with *pentheraphobia*; if you hate or fear your stepmother, *novercaphobia*.

If you are possessed by an irrational aversion to politicians, you have *politicophobia*, if to thieves, *kleptophobia*, if to foreigners, *xenophobia*. If these foreigners are English, you've got *Anglophobia*, if French, *Gallophobia*, if German, *Teutophobia*, and if Russian, *Russophobia*. And if you break out in a cold sweat at even the thought of going to the dentist, you share with me a condition called *dentophobia*.

In addition to the various fears of people, humankind is fraught with terrors of various natural phenomena: *acousticophobia*: noise; *aerophobia*: air; *anemophobia*: cyclones, hurricanes, winds; *antlophobia*: floods; *aquaphobia*: water; *astraphobia*: lightning, thunder; *astrophobia*: stars; *auroraphobia*: northern lights; *blennophobia*: slime; *brontophobia*: thunderstorms; *cheimaphobia*: cold; *chionophobia*: snow; *cometophobia*: comets; *cyrophobia*: frost, ice; *dinophobia*: whirlpools; *elektrophobia*: electricity; *eosophobia*: dawn; *heliophobia*: sun; *homichlophobia*: fog, humidity; *hylophobia*: wood; *lilapsophobia*: tornadoes; *metereophobia*: weather; *nephophobia*: clouds;

Triskaidekaphobia

nyctophobia: darkness; *ombrophobia*: rain; *phengophobia*: daylight; *photophobia*: light; *potomophobia*: rivers; *pyrophobia*: fire; *selaphobia*: flashing light; *skiaphobia*: shadows; *thalassophobia*: the sea; *thermophobia*: heat; *xerophobia*: dry places, like deserts.

When Adam and Eve were expelled from the Garden of Eden, God said to the serpent, "I will put enmity between thee and the woman, and between thy seed and her seed." During its post-Edenic existence, humankind has acquired not only herpetophobia, but so many other fears that up to this point I have listed fewer than half of our named dreads. Naming these terrors may be a kind of magic for holding them at bay. For example, enough people fear the number thirteen that many buildings pretend not to have a thirteenth floor. Still, we assign this affliction a name—*triskaidekaphobia*: *tris*, "three"; *kai*, "and"; *deka*, "ten"; *phobia*, "fear."

In the pages of my local newspaper appeared a story about a woman who for thirty years was held prisoner in her apartment by *agoraphobia*, an intense fear of the outdoors and of open spaces that affects nearly two million Americans. Incredible as it may seem, there is even a label for the fear of getting peanut butter stuck to the roof of the mouth. It is called *arachibutyrophobia*.

Here are a hundred and twenty-five more words that describe the terrors that go bump in our minds:

acrophobia: heights
aichurophobia: being touched by pointed objects
algophobia: pain
alychiphobia: failure
amathophobia: dust

amaxophobia: riding in vehicles
ambulophobia: walking
anuptaphobia: staying single
asthenophobia: weakness
ataxiophobia: disorder
automysophobia: being dirty
ballistrophobia: being shot
basophobia: standing (for fear of falling)
bathophobia: depth
bibliophobia: books
blenophobia: pins and needles
bogyphobia: demons and goblins
bromidrosophobia: body smells
cainophobia: novelty
cardiophobia: heart disease
cathisophobia: sitting
catophtrophobia: mirrors
cherophobia: gaiety
chrematophobia: wealth
chromophobia: colors
chronophobia: time
cibophobia: food
claustrophobia: enclosed spaces
climacophobia: staircases
coitophobia: sexual intercourse
coprophobia: excrement
cremnophobia: precipices
crystallophobia: glass
deipnophobia: dining and dining conversation
demophobia: crowds
diplopiaphobia: double vision
diplychiphobia: accidents

domatophobia: being in a house
dromophobia: crossing streets
dysmorphophobia: deformity
ecophobia: home
emetophobia: vomiting
ergasophobia: work
erotophobia: sexual feelings
erythrophobia: blushing, the color red
eurotophobia: female genitals
febriphobia: fever
gamophobia: marriage
gephyrophobia: crossing bridges
gerascophobia: growing old
glossophobia: speaking in public
graphophobia: writing
gymnophobia: nudity
hagiophobia: saints and the holy
halophobia: speaking
hamartophobia: error or sin
haphephobia: touching, being touched
hedenophobia: pleasure
hematophobia: the sight of blood
hodophobia: travel
homilophobia: sermons
kenophobia: large, empty spaces
kinesophobia: motion
kopophobia: mental or physical examination
laliophobia: talking
lepraphobia: leprosy
linonophobia: string
lygophobia: dark
lyssiophobia: becoming mad

macrophobia: long waits
maieusiophobia: childbirth
mehalophobia: large things
merinthophobia: being bound
metrophobia: poetry
molysomophobia: infection
monophobia: being alone
motorphobia: motor vehicles
musicophobia: music
nosophobia: becoming ill
odontophobia: teeth, especially those of animals
ochlophobia: crowds
odynophobia: pain
oenophobia: wine
olfactophobia: smells
onomatophobia: a certain word or name
opthalmophobia: being stared at
papaphobia: the pope or the papacy
paralipophobia: responsibility
paraphobia: sexual perversion
parthenophobia: young girls
peccatiphobia: sinning
pedophobia: dolls
peniaphobia: poverty
phagophobia: eating or swallowing
pharmacophobia: drugs
philophobia: falling in love or being loved
pnigophobia: choking
ponophobia: fatigue
rhabdophobia: criticism, punishment, being beaten
rhytiphobia: getting wrinkles
scriptophobia: writing

siderodromophobia: train travel
sociophobia: friendship, society
sophophobia: knowledge
spectrophobia: looking in the mirror
stasiphobia: standing
staurophobia: cross or crucifix
stenophobia: narrow places
stygiophobia: hell
tacophobia: speed
taphephobia: cemeteries, being buried alive
tapinophobia: small things
teleophobia: religious ceremonies
telephonophobia: using the telephone
thanatophobia: death, dying
thassophobia: sitting idle
theatrophobia: theaters
theophobia: God
tomophobia: surgical operations
topophobia: certain places
trichophobia: hair
tropophobia: changes
uranophobia: homosexuality
vaccinophobia: vaccines
verbaphobia: words

When Franklin Delano Roosevelt said, in his 1933 inaugural address, "The only thing we have to fear is fear itself," he was warning us against phobophobia, the fear of being afraid. Now that you know that all your phobias have names, you may experience less fear about your fears and about fear itself.

The Secrets of "Nym"

Somebody once defined a synonym as a word you use when you can't spell the word you really want. What a synonym really is, of course, is a word with the same, or nearly the same, meaning as another word, such as *big* and *large* or *small* and *tiny*. Somebody else once quipped that a great many poems seem to have been written by a prolific Irish genius named Ann O'Nymous. Here the pun is on the word *anonymous*, and when a work is anonymous, its creator's name is not revealed.

In *synonym* and *anonymous*, the common element is *onym*, a Greek root that means "word" or "name," and many words about words themselves contain this root. Exploring the secrets of *nym* through a glossary of *nym*ble word words and name words reveals one of the brightest delights of language—its ability to talk about itself:

Ann O'Nymous

Acronym. Coined from two Greek roots that literally mean "high word," acronyms are words made up of the initials of other words. *NASA* is formed from the key letters in National Aeronautics and Space Administration, *radar* from those in radio detecting and ranging, and *SCUBA* from self-contained underwater breathing apparatus. The years since World War II have brought a new refinement to the art of acronyming. This is the reverse acronym, or **bacronym**, in which letters are arranged to form a word that already exists in the language and cleverly underscores some quality of the words that form it. Thus, *ZIP* codes, for "zone improvement plan," reputedly add zip to our mail service, *VISTA* workers (Volunteers In Service To America) provide wider horizons (vistas) for needy Americans, members of *NOW* (National Organization of Women) are in tune with the times, and Mothers Against Drunk Driving are MADD about the tragedies that occur when drinking and driving are mixed.

Anatonym. A part of the body used as a verb: to *toe* the line, *foot* the bill, *face* the music.

Antonym. A word that is opposite in meaning to another word. All *happy* and *sad* takers of the Scholastic Aptitude Test are familiar with this *sweet* and *sour* concept.

Aptronym. A name that is especially suited to the profession of its owner, such as Larry Speakes for a White House spokesperson and Sally Ride for an astronaut. Believe it or not, Dan Druff is a barber, Felicity Foote a dance teacher, and James Bugg an exterminator.

Autonym. A word that describes itself. *Mispelled* is indeed misspelled, and *hippopotomonstrosesquipedalian* is a very long word that means "pertaining to a very long word."

Capitonym. A word that changes pronunciation and meaning when it is capitalized. The name of the town I live in is *Concord*, pronounced "Kahnkerd," while *concord*, lower case and meaning "harmony," is pronounced "kahn-kord." Two shiny examples of capitonyms are "It's time to *polish* the *Polish* tea set" and "After all his suffering, *Job* finally got a *job*." Now sound out this list of my favorite capitonyms in both their lower case and capitalized forms: *askew, august, begin, colon, degas, herb, levy, lima, mobile, natal, nice, rainier, ravel, reading, tangier*.

Charactonym. The name of a literary character that is especially suited to his or her personality. The enormous and enduring popularity of Charles Dickens's works springs in part from the writer's skill at creating memorable charactonyms—Scrooge, the tightfisted miser; Mr. Gradgrind, the tyrannical schoolmaster; Jaggers, the rough-edged lawyer; and Miss Havesham ("have a sham"), the jilted spinster who lives in an illusion.

Modern examples of charactonyms include Willie Loman ("low man") in Arthur Miller's *Death of a Salesman* and Jim Trueblood in Ralph Ellison's *Invisible Man*. Not many years ago, a doctor show named "Marcus Welby" ruled the television ratings. The title of the show and name of the lead character were purposely designed to make us think of "make us well be."

Consonym. Words that have the same pattern of consonants are known as consonyms: *eTHNiC* and *THeNCe*, *SPoNGe* and *eSPioNaGe*.

Domunym. Invented by language maven Paul Dickson, a domunym, literally "home name," is a word used to identify people from particular places: *Philadelphians*, *Rhode Islanders*, *Tacomans*, *Hoosiers*, *Liverpudlians*, *Oxonians*, and *Cantabridgians*.

Euonym. An especially auspicious name, such as the biblical David, "beloved," and Jesus, "savior." English language examples include Harry Truman, Martin Luther King, Jr., and Andrew Marvell.

Exonym. A place name that foreigners use instead of the name that natives use: *Cologne* for Koln, *Florence* for Firenze, *Morocco* for Maroc.

Homonym. A word spelled and pronounced like another word, but of different origin and meaning: *bat* (flying mammal) and *bat* (in baseball), *mint* (an aromatic plant) and *mint* (a place where money is made).

Malonym. A humorous homophone or sound-alike mistake: "In the middle of the field stood a toe-headed boy"; "Our menu is guaranteed to wet your appetite"; "The trouble I'm having with my prostrate gland is making me very tired."

Metonymy. When we use the *crown* to refer to a monarchy, *brass* to refer to military officers, and the *White*

House to refer to the U.S. executive branch, we are in each case employing a metonymy, a name that stands for something else with which it is closely associated. When we call an athlete a *jock*, we make the piece of equipment stand for the person's identity. This metonymy has become so figurative that women can also be jocks.

Patronymic. Family names derived from the father's name or that of a male ancestor are patronymics. *McDonald* means "son of Donald," *O'Grady* "son of Grady," *Johnson* "son of John," and *Richards* "son of Richard."

Pseudonym. The authors of *Alice's Adventures in Wonderland*, *Silas Marner*, and *Nineteen Eighty-Four* have something in common besides being British. They are all better known by their pseudonyms, or pen names, than by their real names. Here are brief biographies of ten famous writers. From the information supplied, can you identify each pseudonym (literally "false name")? You'll find the literary identities on the answer page in the back of this book.

1. Eric Arthur Blair wrote a long fable about a society in which some animals are more equal than others. In 1948 he published a novel about a nightmarish society of the future, one in which everybody had a Big Brother.

2. Samuel Langhorne Clemens was a steamboat pilot before he became a writer. In 1863 he took on the pen name that was a nostalgic reminder of his riverboat days.

3. In March of 1836, what has been described as the most successful writing career in history was launched with the publication of *The Pickwick Papers*. The author, of course, was Charles Dickens. In 1833, when he was only

twenty-one, Dickens began contributing stories and essays to magazines and published them pseudonymously in a collection called *Sketches by* ___________.

4. Charles Lutwidge Dodgson was fascinated with words, logic, and little girls. Out of these interests he fashioned a wonderland of characters—Humpty Dumptys, Jabberwocks, Mad Hatters, and White Rabbits.

5. Famous for her novels describing life in nineteenth-century England, including *Adam Bede*, *Silas Marner*, and *Middlemarch*, Mary Ann Evans adopted a masculine pen name, by George.

6. He meant what he said, and he said what he meant, and his books have pleased children one hundred percent. Theodor Geisel conjured up and drew creatures that now exist in the imaginations of generations of children.

7. William Sydney Porter spent almost four years in prison, where he began his career as an immensely popular writer of short stories. Most of his tales are about life in New York and are marked by surprise endings.

8. Late in life, after a long career as a veterinary surgeon, James Alfred Wight began writing books that communicated his profound affection for animals. The titles of two of those books are taken from a hymn that begins, "All things bright and beautiful, all creatures great and small."

9. Jozef Korzeniowski was born in Poland and grew up speaking no English until he was seventeen, yet he became one of the greatest stylists ever to use the English language. A sailor as a youth, Korzeniowski is most famous for his stories and novels of the sea.

10. Hector Hugh Munro was killed in action during World War I. He left behind him the charming, often biting

short stories to which he signed a pseudonym borrowed from *The Rubaiyat*.

Retronym. Coined by Frank Mankiewicz, a retronym is an adjective-noun pairing generated by a change in the meaning of the noun, usually because of technology. What we used to call, simply, "books" we now call *hardcover books* because of the production of paperback books. What was once simply a "guitar" is now an *acoustic guitar* because of the popularity of electric guitars. What was once simply "soap" is now called *bar soap* since the invention of powdered and liquid soaps. And turf is now available both naturally and artificially.

Tautonym. A word composed of two identical parts, such as *tomtom*, *tutu*, and *goody-goody*.

In the next chapters, we'll explore in depth three especially fascinating members of the *nym* family—**eponyms**, **contronyms**, and **heteronyms**.

Brand-New Eponyms

The ancient gods snatched up the souls of those mortals who found favor in their eyes and made them into stars so that they could shine long after their deaths. Many men and women have been similarly gifted with a measure of immortality by having their names transmuted into common English words. Because of some discovery, object, deed, or quality associated with them, these chosen people—noble or petty, adored or abhorred—continue to twinkle in the heavens of the English language long after they have exited the earthly stage. The Greeks had a word for such people—*eponymos*, from which we derive the term *eponym*, meaning "after or upon a name." Stories of the origins of words made from people or places, real or imaginary, are among the richest and most entertaining about our language.

Perhaps the best-known tale of a mortal immortalized is that of John Montagu, the fourth Earl of Sandwich, from whose clever stratagem descends the word *sandwich*. Word has it that Montagu was spending a typical twenty-four-hour stretch at the gaming tables. Unwilling to forsake his cards for a meal, he ordered his servants to bring him, as his only nourishment, slices of beef slapped between slices of bread. Who would have dreamed that a compulsive gambler would go on to become history's greatest salesman of sliced bread?

King Tantalus, one of the vilest of villains in Greek mythology, is one of many literary creations that pulse just as powerfully as their flesh-and-blood counterparts. To degrade the gods and to test their omniscience, Tantalus invited them to a feast at which he planned to serve the body of his young son, Pelops. But the gods discovered the king's wicked ruse, restored the dead boy to life, and devised a punishment for Tantalus to fit his crime.

Tantalus was banished to Hades, where he was condemned to stand forevermore in a sparkling pool of water with boughs of luscious fruit overhead. He is eternally frustrated, for when he stoops to drink, the water drains away through the bottom of the pool, and when he wishes to eat, the branches of fruit sway from his reach. Ever since, when something presents itself temptingly to our view but teases us by remaining just beyond reach, we say that it *tantalizes* us.

Place names have similarly become enshrined in our dictionaries as everyday words. When they first appeared in England at the beginning of the sixteenth century, colorful, fortune-telling wanderers were called *'gypcians* because they were thought to hail from Egypt, when they actually originated in India. Later, *'gypcians* was shortened to *gypsies*, whence comes the verb *gyp* because these itinerants were perceived as great cheats and rascals.

Even cartoon and comic book characters have a place in the Eponyms Hall of Fame. In 1928, Walt Disney gave the world a Mickey—Mickey Mouse. Until the 1940s, when one said "Mickey Mouse," one meant only the all-American rodent who performed heroic deeds and squeaked his undying love for Minnie. Then came World War II and the subsequent flooding of world markets with Mickey Mouse wristwatches. Because these watches were generally cheap affairs, subject to chronic and chronometric mainspring breakdowns, people started associating anything shoddy or trivial with *mickey mouse*, often lowercased, as in "I'm tired of having to do mickey mouse chores."

The pervasive and persuasive influence of mass marketing and advertising has dramatically speeded up the production of eponyms, and the manufacture of common nouns and verbs from brand names has become a burgeoning source of new words in the English language. When a product achieves wide popular appeal, its name may become a lowercase word for all products of its type, not just a particular brand. You might think that manufacturers would be flattered when their creations achieve such universal fame. On the contrary, companies will spend hundreds of thousands of dollars in legal fees to protect their trademarks from falling into the clutches of competitors.

Faced with such a catch-22 possibility, companies must protect and care for their trademarks, or they will be lost. Here is an alphabetical listing of fifty product names that have become somewhat generic but that have survived legal onslaughts and are still registered. If you don't believe me, look on packages containing these items, and you will still see a symbol of their registered status, such as TM or R, following each mark:

Baggies
Band-Aid
Beer Nuts
Brillo Pads
BVDs
Chap Stick
Coca-Cola/Coke
Cuisinart
Dictaphone
Dixie Cups
Fig Newtons
Frigidaire
Frisbee
Hi-Liter
Jeep
Jell-O
Jockey Shorts
Kitty Litter
Kleenex
Kodak
Ko-Rec-Type
Levi's
Life Savers
Liquid Paper
Mack (Truck)
Magic Marker
Miltown
Novocain
NutraSweet
Ping-Pong
Plexiglas
Polaroid
Popsicle
Pop Tarts
Pyrex
Q-Tips
Sanforized
Sanka
Scotch Tape
Sheetrock
Simoniz
Slim Jim
Styrofoam
Technicolor
TV Dinners
Vaseline
Xerox
Walkman
Wiffle Ball
X-Acto

The Cola Wars

Do you talk about xeroxing a document no matter what machine you use to do the photocopying? Beware: anyone who lowercases *xerox* runs the risk of hearing from the Xerox Corporation, which spends more than $100,000 a year to persuade the public not to say or write xerox when they mean "photocopy." The Johnson & Johnson Company writes admonishing letters to any periodical that prints expressions like "band-aid diplomacy" or "band-aid economics." Although *band-aid* has come to stand for any medicinal plastic strip or merely cosmetic remedy, it is a registered trademark and, by law, should be capitalized. And, if you describe any plastic flying disk as a frisbee, you could get whammed by the Wham-O Manufacturing Company of San Gabriel, California. The idea for the plastic saucers came from the aerodynamic pie tins once manufactured by the Frisbie Bakery in Bridgeport, Connecticut, and the name *Frisbee* remains a registered asset.

For decades the Coca-Cola Company has been playing legal hardball to protect its name. While the courts have allowed other purveyors of soft drinks to use the name *Cola* because it is descriptive of the product, the Supreme Court decided in 1930 that the combination Coca-Cola and the clipped form Coke are the exclusive property of the company. In its most celebrated victory, in 1976, Coca-Cola won an injunction against Howard Johnson's restaurant chain for serving HoJo Cola in place of Coke without informing customers who asked for Coca-Cola by name.

It is ironic that the more successful a product, the more likely it is that its name will become an eponym and lose its privileged status as a result of lawsuits by competitors. The name *Zipper*, for example, was coined by the B.F. Goodrich Company in 1913 as the brand name for its slide fastener on overshoes. After numerous bouts in court, the company retained its rights to use the name on footwear, but to what avail? Zippers are everywhere, and *zipper*, now lowercased, belongs to us all. Aspirin, too, was once a brand name, but in 1921 the Bayer Company was deprived of its exclusive rights to the name. In his classic opinion, Judge Learned Hand stated that *aspirin* had become descriptive of the product itself and that consumers did not call the tablet by its chemical name, acetyl salicylic acid.

As a result of other court judgments, the sole rights to *thermos*, *escalator*, *cellophane*, and *yo-yo* slipped away from the King Seely, Otis Elevator, E. I. Du Pont, and F. Duncan companies respectively. Within the past few years the Miller Brewing Company has had to relinquish control of the word *Lite* on low-calorie beer, Parker Brothers has lost its monopoly on the name *Monopoly*, and the Nestlé Company has had to forfeit its exclusive use of the words *Toll House*.

The same fate has befallen other former brand names, such as *brassiere* (I'm not putting you on!), *celluloid*, *corn flakes*, *cube steak*, *dry ice*, *formica*, *heroin*, *kerosene*, *lanolin*, *linoleum*, *linotype*, *milk of magnesia*, *mimeograph*, *pogostick*, *raisin bran*, *shredded wheat*, and *trampoline*. These words have made such a successful journey from uppercase brand name to lowercase noun that it is difficult to believe that they were ever "owned" by a particular outfit. As more and more brand names become common descriptive terms, rather than labels that distinguish particular products, business will increasingly leave its trademark on our all-consuming English language.

Janus-Faced English

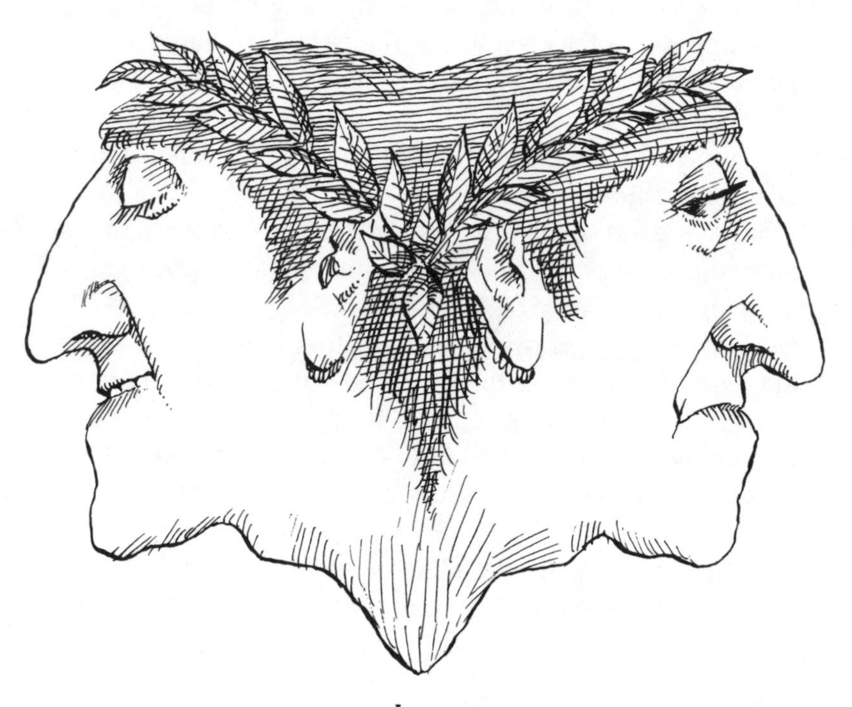

Janus

In the year 1666 a great fire swept through London and destroyed more than half the city, including three quarters of St. Paul's Cathedral. Sir Christopher Wren, the original designer of the Cathedral and perhaps the finest architect of all time, was commissioned to rebuild the great edifice. He began in 1675 and finished in 1710, a remarkably short period of time for such a task. When the magnificent edifice was completed, Queen Anne, the reigning monarch, visited the Cathedral and told Wren that his work was "awful, artificial, and amusing." Sir Christopher, so the story goes, was delighted with the royal compliment, because in those days *awful* meant "full of awe, awe-inspiring," *artificial* meant "artistic," and *amusing*, from the muses, meant "amazing."

That was three hundred years ago. Today, the older, flattering meanings of *awful*, *artificial*, and *amusing* have virtually disappeared from popular use. Indeed, the general rule of language is that when a single word develops two polar meanings, one will become obsolete. Occasionally, though, two diametrically opposed meanings of the same English word survive, and the technical term for these schizophrenics is *contronym*. More popularly, they are known as Janus-faced words because the Greek god Janus had two faces that looked in opposite directions.

Here's a little finger exercise. Remember that I'm the teacher, so you must try to do what I ask. Make a circle with the fingers on your left hand by touching the tip of your index finger to the tip of your thumb. Now poke your head through that circle.

If you unsuccessfully tried to fit your head through the small digital circle, you (and almost any reader) thought that the phrase "poke your head" meant that your head was the poker. But if you raised your left hand with the circle of fingers up close to your forehead and poked your right index finger through that circle until it touched your forehead, you realized that the phrase "poke your head" has a second, and opposite, meaning: that the head is the pokee.

Here are two sentences that will solidify your understanding of how Janus-faced words work:

"The moon is VISIBLE tonight."

"The lights in the old house are always INVISIBLE."

Although the two capitalized words are opposite in meaning, both can be replaced by the same word—*out*. When the moon or sun or stars are out, they are visible. When the lights are out, they are invisible.

Here are some contronymic sentences that show how words wander wondrously and testify to the fact that nothing in the English language is absolute:

with. alongside; against: *a*. England fought with France against Germany. *b*. England fought with France.

clip. fasten; separate: *a*. Clip the coupon to the newspaper. *b*. Clip the coupon from the newspaper.

fast. firmly in one place; rapidly from one place to another: *a*. The pegs held the tent fast. *b*. She ran fast.

bolt. to secure in place; to dart away: *a*. I'll bolt the door. *b*. Did you see the horse bolt?

trim. add things to; cut away: *a*. Let's trim the Christmas tree. *b*. Let's trim the hedge.

dust. remove material from; spread material on: *a*. Three times a week they dust the floor. *b*. Three times each season they dust the crops.

weather. withstand; wear away: *a*. Strong ships weather storms. *b*. Wind can weather rocks.

handicap. advantage, disadvantage: *a*. What's your handicap in golf? *b*. His lack of education is a handicap.

commencement. beginning; conclusion: *a*. Beautiful weather marked the commencement of spring. *b*. She won an award at her high school commencement.

hold up. support; hinder: *a*. Please hold up the sagging branch. *b*. Accidents hold up the flow of traffic.

keep up. continue to fall; continue to stay up: *a*. The farmers hope that the rain will keep up. *b*. Damocles hoped that the sword above his head would keep up.

left. departed from; remaining: *a*. Ten people left the room. *b*. Five people were left in the room.

dress. put items on; remove items from: *a*. Let's dress for the ball. *b*. Let's dress the chicken for cooking.

temper. soften; strengthen: *a*. You must temper your anger with reason. *b*. Factories temper steel with additives.

cleave. separate; adhere firmly: *a*. A strong blow will cleave a plank in two. *b*. Bits of metal cleave to a magnet.

strike. secure in place; remove: *a*. Use a firm grip to strike the nail. *b*. When the show is over, we'll strike the set.

give out. produce; stop producing: *a*. A good furnace will give out enough energy to heat the house. *b*. A broken furnace will often give out.

sanction. give approval of; censure: *a*. The NCAA plans to sanction the event. *b*. Should our country impose a new sanction on Libya?

screen. view; hide from view: *a*. Tonight the critics will screen the film. *b*. Defensemen mustn't screen the puck.

oversight. careful supervision; neglect: *a*. The foreman was responsible for the oversight of the project. *b*. The foreman's oversight ruined the success of the project.

qualified. competent, limited: *a*. The candidate for the job was fully qualified. *b*. The dance was a qualified success.

moot. debatable, not worthy of debate: *a*. Capital punishment is a moot point. *b*. That the earth revolves around the sun is a moot point.

certain. definite, difficult to specify: *a*. I am certain about what I want in life. *b*. I have a certain feeling about the plan.

mortal. deadly, subject to death: *a*. The knight delivered a mortal blow. *b*. All humans are mortal.

a moot point

buckle. fasten together; fall apart: *a*. Safe drivers buckle their seat belts. *b*. Unsafe buildings buckle at the slightest tremor of the earth.

trip. to stumble; to move gracefully: *a*. Don't trip on the curb. *b*. Let's trip the light fantastic.

put out. generate; extinguish: *a*. The candle put out enough light for us to see. *b*. Before I went to bed, I put out the candle.

unbending. rigid; relaxing: *a*. On the job Smith is completely unbending. *b*. Relaxing on the beach is a good way of unbending.

wear. endure through use; decay through use: *a*. This suit will wear like iron. *b*. Water can cause mountains to wear.

scan. examine carefully; glance at hastily: *a*. I scan the poem. *b*. Each day, I scan the want ads.

fix. restore, remove part of: *a*. It's time to fix the fence. *b*. It's time to fix the bull.

seeded. with seeds; without seeds: *a*. The rain nourished the seeded field. *b*. Would you like some seeded raisins?

critical. opposed; essential to: *a*. Joanne is critical of our effort. *b*. Joanne is critical to our effort.

think better. admire more; be suspicious of: *a*. I think better of the first proposal than the second. *b*. If I were you, I'd think better of that proposal.

take. obtain; offer: *a*. Professional photographers take good pictures. *b*. Professional models take good pictures.

impregnable. invulnerable to penetration; able to be impregnated: *a*. The castle was so strongly built that it was impregnable. *b*. Treatments exist for making a childless woman more impregnable.

wind up. start; end: *a*. I have to wind up my watch. *b*. Now I have to wind up this discussion of curious and contrary contronyms.

A Hymn to Heteronyms

Here's a little poem that I've made up. As you read my ditty, note the unusual pattern of end-rhymes:

> Listen, readers, toward me bow.
> Be friendly; do not draw the bow.
> Please don't try to start a row.
> Sit peacefully, all in a row.
> Don't squeal like a big, fat sow.
> Do not the seeds of discord sow.

In the first, third, and fifth lines of this poem, *bow*, *row*, and *sow* all rhyme with *cow* and mean, respectively, "to bend," "argument," and "female pig." In the second, fourth, and sixth lines, *bow*, *row*, and *sow* all rhyme with *low* and mean, respectively, "a weapon," "a line," and "to plant."

Bow, *row*, and *sow* are choice examples of heteronyms--words with the same spelling as other words but with different pronunciations and meanings. Membership in the exclusive club of heteronyms is strict, and tandems such as *resume* and *résumé* and *pate* and *pâté* are not admitted because the accent constitutes a change in spelling. Pseudo-heteronymic pairs like *insult* (noun) and *insult* (verb), *refuse* (noun) and *refuse* (verb), *read* (present-tense verb) and *read* (past-tense verb), and *primer* (beginner's book) and *primer* (base coat of paint) are fairly common in the English language, but they are not true heteronyms because their etymologies are so closely related. True heteronymic pairs that are not clearly related in word formation are among the rarest of occurrences. In each of the following sentences, the heteronyms are italicized. Read each sentence aloud and note what happens to the pronunciations and meanings of each twosome:

After the *slaver* had sold his slaves, he would *slaver* over the money he made.

The *unionized* stockroom workers stacked bottles of ionized and *unionized* solutions.

The storm began to *buffet* the outdoor *buffet*.

The steam-driven *tower* pulled the disabled boat to the lighthouse *tower*.

The *sewer* threw her sewing into the *sewer*.

She is now *resorting* to *resorting* the mail.

He became *resigned* to the fact that he had *resigned* an unfair contract.

Rather than march along sentence by sentence, let's skip along through a poetic hymn to heteronyms:

Please go through the *entrance* of this little poem.
I guarantee it will *entrance* you.
The *content* will certainly make you *content*,
And the knowledge gained sure will enhance you.

A boy *moped* around when his parents refused
For him a new *moped* to buy.
The *incense* he burned did *incense* him to go
On a *tear* with a *tear* in his eye.

He *ragged* on his parents, felt they ran him *ragged*
His just *deserts* they never gave.
He imagined them out on some *deserts* so dry,
Where for water they'd search and they'd rave.

At *present* he just won't *present* or *converse*
On the *converse* of each high-flown theory
Of circles and *axes* in math class; he has
Many *axes* to grind, isn't cheery.

He tried to play baseball, but often *skied* out,
So when the snows came, he just *skied.*
But he then broke a leg *putting* on his ski boots,
And his *putting* in golf was in need.

He once held the *lead* in a cross country race,
'Til his legs started feeling like *lead*.
And when the pain *peaked*, he looked kind of *peaked.*
His *liver* felt *liver*, then dead.

A *number* of times he felt *number*, all *wound*
Up, like one with a *wound*, not a wand.
His new TV *console* just couldn't *console*
Or *slough* off a *slough* of despond.

a bass bass

The *rugged* boy paced 'round his shaggy *rugged* room,
And he spent the whole *evening* 'til dawn
Evening out the cross-*winds* of his hate.
Now my anecdote *winds* on and on.

He thought: "*Does* the prancing of so many *does*
Explain why down *dove* the white *dove*,
Or why *pussy* cat has a *pussy* old sore
And *bass* sing in *bass* notes of their love?"

Do they always sing, "*Do* re mi" and stare, *agape*,
At ease, *agape*, each *minute*?
Their love's not *minute;* there's an *overage* of love.
Even *overage* fish are quite in it.

These bass fish have never been in short *supply*
As they *supply* spawn without waiting.
With their love fluids bubbling, abundant, *secretive*,
There's many a *secretive* mating.

III

Figuratively Speaking

"Prose is a museum where all the old weapons of poetry are kept."

—T. E. Hulme

ENGLISH

A Visit to the Language Zoo

Many children's magazines feature picture puzzles in which the young readers are asked to identify a number of hidden animals. In a cloud may lurk a cow, in the leaves of a tree may be concealed a fish, and on the side of a house may be soaring an eagle. The English language is like those children's pictures. Take a gander at what follows, and you will discover almost three hundred creatures from the animal world hidden in the sentences, a veritable menagerie of zoological metaphors. (Did you catch one of them in the last sentence?)

Human beings, proclaims one dictionary, are distinguished from the other animals "by a notable development of brain with a resultant capacity for speech and abstract reasoning." Perhaps so, but how truly different is our species from our fellow organisms with whom we share the planet?

I mean holy cow, holy cats, and holy mackerel—a little bird told me that the human race is filled with congressional hawks and doves who fight like cats and dogs 'til the cows come home, Wall Street bulls and bears who make a beeline for the goose that lays the golden egg, cold fish and hotdoggers, early birds and night owls, lone wolves and social butterflies, young lions and old crows, and lame ducks, sitting ducks, and dead ducks.

Some people are horny studs on the prowl for other party animals, strutting peacocks who preen and fish for compliments, clotheshorses who put on the dog with their turtlenecks and hush puppies, young bucks and pony-tailed foxy chicks in puppy love who want to get hitched, or cool cats and kittenish lovebirds who avoid stag parties to bill and coo and pet and paw each other in their love nests.

Other people have a whale of an appetite that compels them to eat like pigs (not birds), drink like fish, stuff themselves to the gills, hog the lion's share, and wolf their elephantine portions until they become plump as partridges. Still others are batty, squirrelly, bug-eyed, cock-eyed cuckoos who are mad as march hares and look like something the cat dragged in; crazy as coots, loons, or bedbugs; and who come at us like bats out of hell with their monkeyshines and drive us buggy with their horsing around.

As we continue to separate the sheep from the goats and to pigeonhole the "human" race, we encounter catnapping, slothful sluggards; harebrained jackasses who, like fish out of water, doggedly think at a snail's pace; dumb bunnies and dumb clucks who run around like chickens with their heads cut off; birdbrained dodos who are easily

a lame duck

gulled, buffaloed, and outfoxed; asinine silly gooses who lay an egg whenever, like monkey-see-monkey-do, they parrot and ape every turkey they see; clumsy oxen who are bulls in china shops; and top dogs on their high horses, big fish in small ponds, and cocky bullies high up in the pecking order who rule the roost and never work for chicken feed.

Leapin' lizards, we can scarcely get through a day without meeting crestfallen, pussyfooting chickens who stick their heads in the sand; henpecked underdogs who get goose pimples and butterflies and turn tail; scared rabbits who play possum and cry crocodile tears before they go belly up; spineless jellyfish who clam up with a frog in the throat whenever the cat gets their tongue; mousy worms who quail and flounder and then, quiet as mice, slink off and then return to the fold with their tails between their legs; and shrimpy pipsqueaks who fawn like toadies until you want to croak.

Let's face it. It's a dog-eat-dog world we live in. But doggone it, without beating a dead horse, I do not wish to duck or leapfrog over this subject. It's time to fish or cut bait, to take the bull by the horns, kill two birds with one stone, and, before everything goes to the dogs and we've got a tiger by the tail, to give you a bird's-eye view of the animals hiding in our language.

Dog my cats! It's a bear of a task to avoid meeting catty, shrewish, bitchy vixens with bees in their bonnets whose pet peeve and sacred cow is that all men are swine and chauvinist pigs and in their doghouse. Other brutes who get your goat and ruffle your feathers are antsy, backbiting, crabby, pigheaded old buzzards, coots, and goats who are no spring chickens, who are stubborn as

smelling a rat

mules, and who grouse, bug, badger, dog, and hound you like squawking, droning, waspish gadflies that stir up a hornets' nest and make a mountain out of a molehill.

And speaking of beastly characters that stick in your craw, watch out for the parasites, bloodsuckers, sponges, and leeches who worm their way into your consciousness and make you their scapegoats; the rat finks and stool pigeons who ferret out your deepest secrets and then squeal on you, let the cat out of the bag, and fly the coop without so much as a "Tough turkey. See you later, alligator"; the snakes-in-the-grass who come out of the woodwork, open a can of worms, and then, before you smell a rat, throw you a red herring; the serpentine quacks who make you their gullible guinea pig and cat's-paw; the lowdown curs and dirty dogs who sling the bull, give you a bum steer, and send you on a wild goose chase barking up the wrong tree on a wing and a prayer; the card sharks who hawk their fishy games, monkey with your nest egg, put the sting on you, and then fleece you; the vultures who hang like albatrosses around your neck, who live high on the hog, who feather their own nests and then—the straw that breaks the camel's back—crow about it looking like the cat that swallowed the canary; the black sheep who play cat and mouse and then cook your goose and make a monkey out of you with their shaggy dog stories before they hightail it out of there; and the lousy varmints, polecats, skunks, and eels who sell you a white elephant or a pig in a poke and, when the worm turns and you discover the fly in the ointment, weasel their way out of the deal.

It's a real jungle out there, just one unbridled rat race; in fact, it's for the birds.

But let's talk turkey and horse sense. Don't we go a

tad ape and hog wild over the bright-eyed and bushy-tailed eager beavers who always go whole hog to hit the bull's-eye; the eagle-eyed tigers who are always loaded for bear; and the ducky, loosey-goosey rare birds who are wise as owls and happy as larks and clams? Lucky dogs like these are the cat's pajamas and the cat's meow, worthy of being lionized. From the time they're knee-high to a grasshopper, they're in the catbird seat and the world is their oyster.

So before you buzz off, I hope you'll agree that this exhibit of animal metaphors has been no fluke, no hogwash, no humbug. I really give a hoot about the animals hiding in our English language, so, for my swan song, I want you to know that, straight from the horse's mouth, this has been no dog-and-pony show and no cock-and-bull story.

It really is a zoo out there.

You Said a Mouthful

Now that you have uncovered the hidden herds of animals, flocks of birds, swarms of insects, and universities of fish that metaphorically run, fly, creep, and swim through our English language, it's time to nibble on another spicy, meaty, juicy honey of a topic that I know you'll want to savor and relish. Feast your eyes now on the veritable potpourri of mushrooming food expressions that grace the table of our English language and season our tongue. As we chew the fat about the food-filled phrases that are packed like sardines and sandwiched into our everyday conversations, I'll sweeten the pot with some tidbits of food for thought guaranteed to whet your appetite.

I know what's eating you. I've heard through the grapevine that you don't give a fig because you think I'm nutty as a fruitcake; that you're fed up with me for biting off more than I can chew; that you want me to drop this subject like a hot potato because I'm a spoiled rotten weenie; and that you're giving me the raspberry for asking you to swallow a cheesy, corny, mushy, saccarhine, seedy, soupy, sugarcoated, syrupy topic that just isn't your cup of tea.

I understand that you're beet red with anger that I'm feeding you a bunch of baloney, garbage, and tripe; that I've rubbed salt in your wounds by making you ruminate on a potboiler that's no more than a tempest in a teapot; that I've upset your apple cart by rehashing an old chestnut that's just pie in the sky and won't amount to a hill of beans; that you want to chew me out for putting words in your mouth; that you're boiling and simmering because you think I'm a candy-assed apple polisher who's out to egg you on.

But nuts to all that. That's the way the cookie crumbles. Eat your heart out and stop crying in your beer. I'm going to stop mincing words and start cooking with gas, take my idea off the back burner and bring home the bacon without hamming it up. No matter how you slice it, this fruitful, tasteful topic is the greatest thing since sliced bread, the icing on the cake. Rather than crying over spilt milk and leaping out of the frying pan and into the fire, I'm going to put all my eggs into one basket, take potluck, and spill the beans. I'm cool as a cucumber and confident that this crackerjack, peachy-keen, vintage feast that I've cooked up will have you eating out of the palm of my hand.

I don't wish to become embroiled in a rhubarb, but your beefing and stewing sound like sour grapes from a

pie in the sky

tough nut to crack—kind of like the pot calling the kettle black. But if you've digested the spoonfed culinary metaphors up to this point in this meat-and-potatoes chapter, the rest will be gravy, duck soup, a piece of cake, and easy as pie—just like taking candy from a baby.

Just think of the various people we meet every day. Some have taste. Others we take with a grain of salt. Some drive us bananas and crackers. Still others are absolutely out to lunch:

• the young sprouts and broths of lads who feel their oats and are full of beans;

• the salty, crusty oldsters who are wrinkled as prunes and live to a ripe old age well beyond their salad days;

• the peppery smart cookies (no mere eggheads, they) who use their beans and noodles to cut the mustard;

• the half-baked meat heads, the flaky couch potatoes, and the pudding-headed vegetables who drive us nuts with their slow-as-molasses peabrains and who gum up the works and are always in a pickle, a jam, hot water, the soup, or a fine kettle of fish;

• the unsavory, crummy, hard-boiled, ham-fisted rotten apples with their cauliflower ears, who can cream us, beat the stuffing out of us, make us into mincemeat and hamburger, and knock us ass over teakettle and flatter than a pancake;

• the mealymouthed marshmallows, Milquetoasts, milksops, half-pints, and cream puffs who walk on eggshells and whose knees turn to jelly as they gingerly waffle and fudge on every issue to see which side their bread is buttered on;

• the carrot-topped, pizza-faced string beans and bean

top banana

poles who, with their lumpy Adam's apples, are long drinks of water;

• the top bananas, big cheeses, and big breadwinners who ride the gravy train by making a lot of lettuce and dough and who never work for peanuts or small potatoes;

• the honeys, tomatoes, dumplings, cheesecakes, and sweetie pies with their peaches-and-cream complexions, strawberry blond hair, almond eyes, and cherry lips;

• the saucy tarts who wiggle their melons and buns and fritter away their time buttering up their meal tickets and milking their sugar daddies dry;

• the salt-of-the-earth good eggs who take the cake, know their onions, make life a bowl of cherries, and become the apples of our eye and the toasts of the town.

Hot dog! I hope you're pleased as punch that this souped-up topic is a plum, not a lemon: the berries, not the pits. The proof of the pudding is in the eating, and this cream of the crop of palate-pleasing food figures is bound to sell like hotcakes. I'm no glutton for punishment for all the tea in China, but, if I'm wrong, I'll eat crow and humble pie. I don't wish to take the words right out of your mouth, but, in a nutshell, it all boils down to the fact that every day we truly eat our words.

Violent English

Everyone deplores violence these days. Many articles and books, radio and television programs, and self-help and encounter groups are designed to help us curb our tempers. And with the specters of international terrorism and nuclear warfare haunting our horizon, it may be that the future of the human race depends upon our ability to channel our violent impulses and to locate solutions based on cooperation rather than aggression.

When we *tackle*, *wrestle*, and *grapple* with the problem of violence, we are bound to be *struck* by a crucial idea. If our view of reality is shaped and defined by the words and phrases we use, then violence is locked deep in our thoughts, frozen in the clichés and expressions of everyday life. "I'll be *hanged*!" we are likely to exclaim as this insight *hits* us with a *vengeance*. "I believe that I've *hit* the nail right on the head!"

"I'll be hanged!"

twisting someone's arm

Let's take a *stab* at the issue of violence in our everyday parlance with a *crash* course on the words we use to describe disagreements. First, we *rack* our brains assembling an *arsenal* of arguments. Then we attempt to *demolish* the opposition's points with a *barrage* of criticism, *attack* their positions by *nailing them dead to rights*, *letting them have it with both barrels*, and *shooting down* their contentions. We *break* their concentration by *puncturing* their assumptions, *cut them down to size* by *hammering* away at their weaknesses, *torpedo* their efforts with *barbed* criticism, and then, when *push* comes to *shove*, *assault* their integrity with character *assassination*. If all else fails, we try to *twist their arms* and *kill* them with kindness.

Now we can begin to understand the full *impact* of the expression "to have a *violent disagreement*."

The world of business is a veritable *jungle* of *cutthroat* competition, a *rough-and-tumble* school of *hard knocks*, and a *dog-eat-dog* world of *backbiting*, *backstabbing*, and *hatchet* jobs. Some companies *spearhead* a trend of price *gouging*. Other firms *beat* the competition to the *punch* and gain a *stranglehold* on the market by *fighting tooth and nail* to *slash* prices in *knock-down-drag-out*, *no-holds-barred* price *wars*. Still other companies gain *clout* by putting the *squeeze* on their competitors with *shakeups*, *raids*, and *hostile takeovers*. Then the other side gets *up in arms* and *screams bloody murder* about such a *low blow*.

No wonder that business executives are often recruited by *headhunters*. No wonder that *bleeding hearts* who can't *fight their own battles* are likely to get *axed*, *booted*, *canned*, *discharged*, *dumped*, *fired*, *kicked out*, *sacked*, or *terminated*.

One would hope that sporting contests would provide an escape from life's daily *grind*. But once again we find mayhem and havoc embedded in the adversarial expressions of matters athletic. In fact, we can't get within *striking* distance of a big game without *running* or *bumping* into some ticket *scalper* who's out to *rip us off* and get away with *murder*. Once inside the stadium or arena, we witness two teams trying to *battle*, *beat*, *clobber*, *crush*, *dominate*, *maul*, *pulverize*, *rout*, *slaughter*, *steamroll*, *thrash*, *throttle*, *wallop*, *whip*, *wipe out*, *kick the pants off*, *make mincemeat out of*, *stick it to*, and *wreak havoc on* each other with *battle plans* that include *suicide squeezes*, *grand slams*, *blitzes*, *shotgun offenses*, *aerial bombs*, *punishing ground attacks*, and *slam dunks*. Naturally both sides hope that they won't *choke* in *sudden death* overtime.

Fleeing the battlefields of athletics at *breakneck* speed, we seek release from our violent language by taking in some entertainment. We look to *kill* some time at a *dynamite* show that's supposed to be a *smash hit blockbuster* and a *slapstick riot* that we'll get a *kick* and a *bang* out of. But the whole *shootin'* match turns out to be a *bomb* and a *dud*, rather than a *blast* and a *bash*.

The lead may be a *knockout* and *stunning bombshell*, but she *butchers* her lines and her *clashing* outfit *grates* on our nerves. Sure as *shootin'*, we're *burned up* and bored to *death* with the sheer *torture* of it all. We feel like *tearing* our hair out, *eating our heart out*, *gnashing* our teeth, *snapping* at others, and *kicking* ourselves. So, all *bent out of shape*, we go off *half-cocked* and *beat* it home feeling like *battered*, *heartbroken* nervous *wrecks*. The situation is *explosive*. We've been through the *meat grinder*, and we're ready to *blow* our tops and stacks, *shoot* off our mouths, *wring* somebody's neck, *knock* his block and socks off, and go on the *warpath*. We've got a real axe to grind.

Even alcohol and drugs won't offer any releases from the prison of violence in which we English speakers are incarcerated. However *blitzed*, *bombed*, *hammered*, *plowed*, *smashed*, *stoned*, or *wasted* we become, we must eventually *crash*. It's like using a double-edged *sword* to *cut off* our nose to spite our face.

If language is truly a window to the world and if the words and expressions we use truly affect the way we think, can we ever really stamp out violence?

IV

Unmechanical English

"English usage is sometimes more than mere taste, judgment, and education. Sometimes it's sheer luck, like getting across the street."

—E. B. WHITE

Farmer Pluribus

Foxen in the Henhice

Recently I undertook an extensive study of American dialects, and a friend told me about a farmer named Eben Pluribus who spoke a most unusual kind of English. So I went to visit Farmer Pluribus, and here is a transcript of our interview:

"Mr. Pluribus, I hear that you've had some trouble on the farm."

"Well, young fella, times were hard for a spell. Almost every night them danged foxen were raiding my henhice."

"Excuse me, sir," I interjected. "Don't you mean foxes?"

"Nope, I don't," Pluribus replied. "I use oxen to plow my fields, so it's foxen that I'm trying to get rid of."

"I see. But what are henhice?" I asked.

"Easy. One mouse, two mice; one henhouse, two henhice. You must be one of them city slickers, but surely you know that henhice are what them birds live in that, when they're little critters, they utter all them peep."

"I think I'm beginning to understand you, Mr. Pluribus. But don't you mean peeps?"

"Nope, I mean peep. More than one sheep is a flock of sheep, and more than one peep is a bunch of peep. What do you think I am, one of them old ceet?"

"I haven't meant to insult you, sir," I gulped. "But I can't quite make out what you're saying."

"Then you must be a touch slow in the head," Farmer Pluribus shot back. "One foot, two feet; one coot, two ceet. I'm just trying to easify the English language, so I make all regular plural nouns irregular. Once they're all irregular, then it's just the same like they're all regular."

"Makes perfect sense to me," I mumbled.

"Good boy," said Pluribus, and a gleam came into his eyes. "Now, as I was trying to explain, them pesky foxen made such a fuss that all the meese and lynges have gone north."

"Aha!" I shouted. "You're talking about those big antlered animals, aren't you? One goose, two geese; one moose, a herd of meese. And lynges is truly elegant—one sphinx, a row of sphinges; one lynx, a litter of lynges."

"You're a smart fella, sonny," smiled Pluribus. "You see, I used to think that my cose might scare away them foxen, but the cose were too danged busy chasing rose."

"Oh, oh. You've lost me again," I lamented. "What are cose and rose?"

"Guess you ain't so smart after all," Pluribus sneered.

"If *those* is the plural of *that*, then *cose* and *rose* got to be the plurals of *cat* and *rat*."

"Sorry that I'm so thick, but I'm really not one of those people who talk through their hose," I apologized, picking up Pluribus's cue. "Could you please tell me what happened to the foxen in your henhice?"

"I'd be pleased to," answered Pluribus. "What happened was that my brave wife, Una, grabbed one of them frying pen and took off after them foxen."

I wondered for a moment what frying pen were and soon realized that because the plural of *man* is *men*, the plural of *pan* had to be *pen*.

"Well," Pluribus went right on talking, "the missus wasn't able to catch them foxen so she went back to the kitchen and began throwing dish and some freshly made pice at them critters."

That part of the story stumped me for a time, until I reasoned that a school of fish is made up of fish and more than one die make a roll of dice so that Una Pluribus must have grabbed a stack of dishes and pies.

Pluribus never stopped. "Them dish and pice sure scarified them foxen, and the pests have never come back. In fact, the rest of the village heard about what my wife did, and they were so proud that they sent the town band out to the farm to serenade her with tubae, harmonicae, accordia, fives, and dra."

"Hold up!" I gasped. "Give me a minute to figure out those musical instruments. The plural of *formula* is *formulae*, so the plurals of *tuba* and *harmonica* must be *tubae* and *harmonicae*. And the plurals of *phenomenon* and *criterion* are *phenomena* and *criteria*, so the plural of *accordion* must be *accordia*."

"You must be one of them genii," Pluribus exclaimed.

"Maybe," I blushed. "One cactus, two cacti; one alumnus, an association of alumni. So one genius, a seminar of genii. But let me get back to those instruments. The plurals of *life* and *wife* are *lives* and *wives*, so the plural of *fife* must be *fives*. And the plural of *medium* is *media*, so the plural of *drum* must be *dra*. Whew! That last one was tough."

"Good boy, sonny. Well, my wife done such a good job of chasing away them foxen that the town newspaper printed up a story and ran a couple of photographim of her holding them pen, dish, and pice."

My brain was now spinning in high gear, so it took me but an instant to realize that Farmer Pluribus had regularized one of the most exotic plurals in the English language—seraph, seraphim; so photograph, photographim. I could imagine all those Pluribi bathing in their bathtubim, as in cherub, cherubim; bathtub, bathtubim.

"Well," crowed Pluribus. "I was mighty pleased that everybody was so nice to the missus, but that ain't no surprise since folks in these here parts show a lot of respect for their methren."

"Brother, brethren; mother, methren," I rejoined. "That thought makes me want to cry. Have you any boxen of Kleenices here?"

"Sure do, young fella. And I'm tickled pink that you've caught on to the way I've easified the English language. One index, two indices and one appendix, two appendices. So one Kleenex, two Kleenices. Makes things simpler, don't it?"

I was so grateful to Farmer Pluribus for having taught me his unique dialect that I took him out to one of them local cafeteriae. Then I reported my findings to the American Dialect Society by calling from one of the telephone beeth in the place.

Yep, you've got it. One tooth, two teeth. One telephone booth, two telephone beeth. Makes things simpler, don't it?

Tense Times with Verbs

Have you heard the one about the man who went to trial for having pulled a woman down a street by the hair? When the judge asked the arresting officer, "Was she drugged?" the policeman answered, "Yes sir, a full block." Or the one about the woman who asked a Boston cab driver where she could get scrod. "I didn't know that the verb had that past tense," muttered the cabbie.

Both jokes rely on the fact that verb tenses in English are crazy, fraught with a fearful asymmetry and puzzling unpredictability. Some verbs form their past tense by adding *-d*, *-ed*, or *-t*—*walk*, *walked*; *bend*, *bent*. Others go back in time through an internal vowel change—*begin*, *began*; *sing*, *sang*. Another cluster adds *-d* or *-t* and undergoes an internal vowel change—*lose*, *lost*; *buy*, *bought*. And still others don't change at all—*set*, *set*; *put*, *put*. No

"I didn't know that the verb had that past tense."

wonder, then, that our eyes glaze and our breath quickens when we have to form the past tense of verbs like *dive*, *weave*, *shine*, *sneak*, and *baby-sit*.

The past tenses of verbs in our language cause so many of us to become tense that I've written a poem about the insanity:

The verbs in English are a fright.
How can we learn to read and write?
Today we speak, but first we spoke;
Some faucets leak, but never loke.
Today we write, but first we wrote;
We bite our tongues, but never bote.

Each day I teach, for years I taught,
And preachers preach, but never praught.
This tale I tell; this tale I told;
I smell the flowers, but never smold.

If knights still slay, as once they slew,
Then do we play, as once we plew?
If I still do as once I did,
Then do cows moo, as they once mid?

I love to win, and games I've won;
I seldom sin, and never son.
I hate to lose, and games I lost;
I didn't choose, and never chost.

I love to sing, and songs I sang;
I fling a ball, but never flang.
I strike that ball, that ball I struck;
This poem I like, but never luck.

I take a break, a break I took;
I bake a cake, but never book.
I eat that cake, that cake I ate;
I beat an egg, but never bate.

I often swim, as I once swam;
I skim some milk, but never skam.
I fly a kite that I once flew;
I tie a knot, but never tew.

I see the truth, the truth I saw;
I flee from falsehood, never flaw.
I stand for truth, as I once stood;
I land a fish, but never lood.

About these verbs I sit and think.
These verbs don't fit. They seem to wink
At me, who sat for years and thought
Of verbs that never fat or wought.

I beat an egg, but never bate.

Spellbound

In 1750, Phillip, Fourth Earl of Chesterfield, wrote, in a letter to his son, "One false spelling may fix a stigma upon a man for life." If Lord Chesterfield's chilling dictum is true, all of us are stigmatized, for who among us has not stumbled into the potholes and booby traps that dot the terrain of English orthography?

Indeed, with the possible exceptions of sports commissioners and unsuccessful presidential candidates, there is no more popular object of abuse and ridicule than our "system" of English spelling. Once, when trying to write a Presidential paper, Andrew Jackson blew his stack and cried, "It's a damn poor mind that can think of only one way to spell a word!" Linguists Otto Jespersen and Mario Pei offer more professional pronouncements: Spelling is a "pseudohistorical and antieducational abomination" that is "the world's most awesome mess."

These are strong words, but even the briefest glance at the situation reveals that they are quite just. In what other language can one find the pairs *publicly* and *basically*, *four* and *forty*, *float* and *flotation*, *led* and *read* (past tense), *harass* and *embarrass*, *deceit* and *receipt*? In what other language can *manslaughter* and *man's laughter* be spelled with exactly the same letters? In what other language can *coffee* be misspelled *kauphy* and *usage*, *yowzitch*—not a single correct letter in the bunch!

Long ago T. S. Watt published a poem titled "English" in the *Manchester Guardian*:

> I take it you already know
> Of *tough* and *bough* and *cough* and *dough*?
> Others may stumble, but not you
> On *hiccough*, *thorough*, *lough*, and *through*.
> Well done! And now you wish, perhaps,
> To learn of less familiar traps?
>
> Beware of *heard*, a dreadful word
> That looks like *beard* and sounds like *bird*.
> And *dead:* it's said like *bed*, not *bead*—
> For goodness' sake don't call it "deed"!
> Watch out for *meat* and *great* and *threat*.
> (They rhyme with *suite* and *straight* and *debt*.)
> A moth is not a moth in *mother*,
> Nor *both* in *bother*, *broth* in *brother*,
> And *here* is not a match for *there*,
> Nor *dear* and *fear* for *bear* and *pear*,
> And then there's *dose* and *rose* and *lose*

Just look them up—and *goose* and *choose*,
And *cork* and work and *card* and *ward*,
And *font* and *front* and *word* and *sword*,
And *do* and *go* and *thwart* and *cart*—
Come, come, I've hardly made a start!

A dreadful language? Man alive!
I'd mastered it when I was five.
And yet to write it, the more I tried,
I hadn't learned at fifty five.

The most prominent cause of all this whoop-de-do (also whoop-de-doo) about English orthography is the considerable distance that stretches between the sounds of our words and their spelling—a state of affairs created by the inadequacy of our Roman alphabet to represent all the sounds of English; our cheerful willingness to borrow words and, with them, unconventional sounds from other languages; and, finally, the gradual changes in the way we pronounce words, most of which have not been matched by repairs to our spelling. The result is that about eighty percent of our words are not spelled phonetically. In effect, we have two languages, one spoken and one written.

One way to explore the chasm that divides phonology from orthography is to examine how letters, alone or in combination, can represent a variety of disparate sounds. The *e*'s in *reentered*, for example, have four different pronunciations, including one silent letter. A favorite target of the scoffers is the letter string *ough*, a terror that can produce at least ten distinct sounds, as in *bough*, *bought*, *cough*, *dough*, *hiccough*, *lough*, *rough*, *thoroughbred*, *through*, and *trough*. Further evidence that letters do not

TOTI
EMUL
ESTO

represent specific sounds comes from the story about a sign a GI saw on a post in Italy during World War II:

T O T I
E M U L
E S T O

What did the sign spell? "TO TIE MULES TO."

What most complicates the situation is that English spelling is haunted by what William Watt calls "the little ghosts of silent letters." Indeed, it has been estimated that two thirds of our lexicon is populated with these mischievous specters, leading Thorstein Veblen to proclaim: "English orthography satisfies all the requirements of the canons of reputability under the law of conspicuous waste."

Confronted by such delicious chaos, the intrepid logophile is moved to ask: Are there contexts in which all twenty-six letters in the alphabet are mute? I believe that the answer is "yes" and offer this lineup, with multiple settings wherever possible, to demonstrate the deafening silence that rings through English orthography:

A: algae, bread, marriage, pharaoh

B: doubt, thumb

C: blackguard, Connecticut, indict, science

D: edge, handkerchief, Wednesday

E: height, hope, steak, yeoman

F: halfpenny

G: gnome, reign, tight

H: bough, ghost, honor, rhyme

I: bait, business, thief, Sioux

J: rijsttafel

K: blackguard, know

L: halfpenny, Lincoln, salmon, would

M: mnemonic

N: column

O: country, laboratory, people, tortoise

P: cupboard, pneumonia, psychiatry, receipt

Q: racquet

R: forecastle, Worcester

S: aisle, debris, island, rendezvous

T: gourmet, listen, parfait, rapport

George Bernard Shaw

U: circuit, dough, gauge, guide

V: flivver, savvy

W: answer, cockswain, two, wrist

X: faux pas, grand prix, Sioux

Y: aye, crayon

Z: pince-nez, rendezvous*

Now let us reverse our field. Not only can certain letters represent a variety of sounds (and silences); we also find that a single sound can be recorded by many different letters. George Bernard Shaw, who first championed and then bequeathed a sizable (also sizeable) sum of money to the cause of spelling reform, once announced that he had discovered a new way to spell the word *fish*. His fabrication was *ghoti: gh* as in enou*gh*, *o* as in w*o*men, and *ti* as in na*ti*on. But there are many other "fish" in the sea—*phusi*: *ph* as in *ph*ysic, *u* as in b*u*sy, *si* as in pen*si*on; *ffess:* o*ff*, pr*e*tty, i*ss*ue; *ughyce:* la*ugh*, h*y*mn, o*ce*an; *Pfeechsi:* *Pf*eiffer, b*ee*n, fu*chsi*a; *pphiapsh: sapph*ire, marr*ia*ge, *psh*aw; *fuise:* *f*at, gu*i*lt, nau*se*ous; *ftaisch:*

*I would welcome suggestions for improving any of the above items, especially the following: *J: rijsttafel* (pronounced *reestahfull*), an Indonesian rice dish, has other *ij* analogies, such as nijmegan and *rijksdaalder*, but I would prefer something that sounds more "native." *Q:* in *racquet* I am forced to contend that either the *c* or the *qu* is silent, with no basis for choosing which one. *V:* for this most elusive letter in my search, I can uncover only double-letter examples such as those listed above. This is not entirely satisfactory, as double letters can easily be found for almost every letter in the alphabet—*aardvark*, *babble*, etc.

*soft*en, vill*ain*, *sch*wa; *ueisci:* lieu*t*enant, forf*eit*, con*sci*ous. We stop here only because the game has become "in-*f*-able."

We can adapt Shaw's tactic to almost any word. My last name, for instance, can be represented by *Lleoddo-loyrrh*, a Frankenstein's monster sewn together from the pieces of ba*ll*, *leo*pard, bla*dd*er, co*lo*nel, and m*yrrh*. In fact, in studying phoneme-grapheme correspondences, I have become such a Wizard of *Oh*s that I can now unveil a twenty-one word sentence in which every word contains a long *oh* sound, yet each is spelled differently: "Although yeoman folk owe Pharaoh's Vaud bureau hoed oats, chauvinistic van Gogh, swallowing cognac oh so soulfully, sews grosgrained, picoted, brooched chapeaux."

Now perhaps you can understand the logic behind the Rolaids commercial that asks, "How do you spell relief?" Then you see a clown or some other stooge writing on a mirror or blackboard the answer: R-O-L-A-I-D-S.

Given the "awesome mess" of English spelling, the Rolaids people may have a point.

V

The Sounds of English

"Spanish is the language for lovers, Italian for singers, French for diplomats, German for horses, and English for geese."

—Spanish proverb

Sound and Sense

What do these words have in common: *bash*, *clash*, *crash*, *dash*, *gash*, *gnash*, *hash*, *lash*, *mash*, *slash*, *smash*, *thrash*, and *trash*?

"The words all rhyme," you answer.

Right. But can you spot what it is that the thirteen words share in their content?

Faces are bashed, gashed, slashed, and smashed. Cars crash. Hopes are dashed. Enemies clash. Teeth gnash. Beef is hashed. Potatoes are mashed. Rooms are trashed. And prisoners are lashed and thrashed.

Now the pattern becomes clearer. All of these *-ash* words are verbs that express terrible actions of great violence. Why, over the more than 1500-year history of the English language, have speakers seized on the *-ash* sound cluster to create words that describe mutilation?

Listen closely to the broad *a*, and you will hear that it sounds like a drawn-out human scream. Now listen closely to the hissing sound of *sh*, and note that it too takes a long time to expel. The eighteenth-century English poet Alexander Pope once wrote that "The sound must seem an echo of the sense." It appears that the agonizing, hissy, drawn-out sound of *-ash* is particularly well suited to the sense of violent actions that unfold over seconds, minutes, or even longer periods of time.

The ancient Greek philosophers Pythagoras (whose theorem of the right triangle we confront in geometry classes), Heraclitus, and Plato subscribed to what many now call the ding-dong theory of language origin. They believed that the universe is like a great bell and that every object in nature has a special "ring." Strike an object and out comes a word the sound of which is inherent in the thing itself.

"Balderdash!" you respond, uttering another mutilative *-ash* word. "Such an a priori correspondence between sound and sense can't possibly exist. Only human beings can invent words; syllables can't repose in things themselves." But, keeping an open mind (rather than a hole in the head), consider the evidence for the validity of the ding-dong theory of word formation.

Let's start with initial consonant sounds:

The word for *mother* (and *mama* and *mom*) in most languages begins with the letter *m*: *mater* (Latin), *mère* (French), *madre* (Spanish), *Mutter* (German), *mam* (Welsh), *mat* (Russian), and *masake* (Crow Indian). Could it be more than mere coincidence that this pervasive *m* sound for words maternal is made by the pursing of lips in the manner of the suckling babe?

the ding-dong theory

Think of all the words you know that begin with *fl-*. Your list will probably include the likes of *flicker*, *flutter*, *flurry*, *flip*, *flap*, *fly*, *flow*, *flash*, *flee*, *flare*, *fling*, *flush*, *flame*, *flail*, and *flounce*. Could the fact that the tongue darts forward whenever we form *fl-* in our mouths account for the sense of movement, usually rapid movement, in all of these words?

Why do so many words beginning with *sn-* pertain to the nose: *snot*, *sneeze*, *snort*, *snore*, *sniff*, *sniffle*, *snuff*, *snuffle*, *snarl*, *snivel*, *snoot*, *snout*, *sneer*, and *snicker*? And why are so many other *sn-* words distasteful and unpleasant: *sneak*, *snide*, *snob*, *snitch*, *snit*, *snub*, *snafu*, *snoop*, *snipe*, *snake*, and *snaggle tooth*? To appreciate the nasal aggression inherent in *sn-*, form the sound and note how your nose begins to wrinkle, your nostrils flare, and your lips draw back to expose your threatening canine teeth.

Think for a moment of how forcibly the sound of an initial *b* is expelled as it flies from the lips like a watermelon seed. Then observe how many words beginning with that letter denote the expulsion of breath—*breathe*, *blow*, *blab*, *blather*, *bluster*, *babble*, *bloviate*, and *blubber*—or the application of force—*batter*, *blast*, *bang*, *bust*, *bruise*, *bludgeon*, *bump*, *break*, *butt*, *beat*, *bash*, *bounce*, and *bomb*.

Listen now to the sounds of vowels in the middle of words:

What happens to the pattern of internal vowels in strong, irregular verbs: *sing*, *sang*, *sung*; *ring*, *rang*, *rung*? Place your thumb and forefinger on your Adam's apple as you say these words aloud and you will notice that, as the verbs move backwards in time (today I sing, yesterday I sang, for years I have sung), the vowels themselves echo the process by traveling back in the throat.

Consider the short *i* vowel in words like *little*, *kid*, *slim*, *thin*, *skinny*, *imp*, *shrimp*, *midget*, *pygmy*, and *piddling*. What do these words have in common? They all denote smallness or slightness. Why? Perhaps because, when we pronounce the short *i*, we tighten our lips together and make our mouths small.

Now that you are opening your ears to sound and sense, consider these questions about a few sounds that come at the ends of words:

Why is it that many words ending with *-ng* echo with metallic resonance: *bong*, *boing*, *gong*, *ping*, *ring*, *clang*, and *ding-dong*?

Why is it that the final voiceless stops *p*, *t*, and *k* come at the end of quick-action words, like *pop*, *clip*, *snip*, *snap*, *rap*, *tap*, *slap*, *whip*, *pat*, *cut*, *slit*, *hit*, *dart*, *flit*, *crack*, *click*, *flick*, *smack*, *whack*, *strike*, and *peck*? Robert Browning put this pattern to sensitive use in "Meeting at Night":

> A *tap* at the pane, the *quick sharp* scratch
> And blue *spurt* of a lighted match

Why are almost all words that end with *-unk* unpleasant in their suggestions: *clunk*, *junk*, *punk*, *drunk*, *dunk*, *skunk*, *stunk*, *flunk*, *bunk*, *lunk*, *funk*, and *gunk*?

Why do so many words ending with *-ush* have to do with water: *flush*, *gush*, *lush*, *mush*, *rush*, *slush*, and (*orange*) *crush*?

Why does the following cluster of *-allow* words convey qualities that indicate a lack of something? A *callow* youth

rotund egghead

lacks experience, a *fallow* field lacks use, a *sallow* complexion lacks color, and a *shallow* mind lacks depth.

As a final example, why do so many words ending in *-ump* suggest a round mass: *clump*, *rump*, *lump*, *bump*, *mumps*, *plump*, *hump*, *stump*, and *chump* (originally a short, thick piece of wood)? No wonder the great wordsmith and creator of children's stories, Lewis Carroll, named his rotund egghead *Humpty Dumpty*. Now there's a writer who could really hear and feel the sounds of English words.

Beautiful English

Mark Twain plunked the following description into the middle of his "Double-Barreled Detective Story." Read the passage and reflect on the power of beautiful English words:

"It was a crisp and spicy morning in early October. The lilacs and laburnums, lit with the glory-fires of autumn, hung burning and flashing in the upper air, a fairy bridge provided by kind Nature for the wingless wild things that have their homes in the tree-tops and would visit together; the larch and the pomegranate flung their purple and yellow flames in brilliant broad splashes along the slanting sweep of the woodland; the sensuous fragrance of innumerable deciduous flowers rose upon the swooning atmosphere; far in the empty sky a solitary esophagus slept upon motionless wing; everywhere brooded stillness, serenity, and the peace of God."

Did the mellifluous lilting of Twain's prose beguile you into overlooking the basic meaninglessness of the passage, including the absurd sleeping esophagus?

More than fifty years ago, a poll was conducted among American writers to ascertain which English words they considered to be the "most beautiful" in the language. In replying to the question, Louis Untermeyer, the poet and critic, wrote, "The most musical words seem to be those containing the letter *l*. I think, offhand, of such words as *violet*, *lake*, *laughter*, *willow*, *lovely*, and other such *l*impid and *l*iquid sy*ll*ables."

Dr. Wilfred Funk, a famous tracker of word origins, chose *tranquil*, *golden*, *hush*, *bobolink*, *thrush*, *lullaby*, *chimes*, *murmuring*, *luminous*, *damask*, *cerulean*, *melody*, *marigold*, *jonquil*, *oriole*, *tendril*, *myrrh*, *mignonette*, *gossamer*, *fawn*, *dawn*, *chalice*, *anemone*, *mist*, *oleander*, *amaryllis*, *rosemary*, *camellia*, *asphodel*, and *halcyon*.

Lowell Thomas selected *home*, Irvin S. Cobb *Chattanooga*, Charles Swain Thomas *melody*, Stephen D. Wise *granobility*, Lew Sarett *vermilion*, Bess Streeter Aldrich *gracious*, Arnold Bennett *pavement*, George Balch Nevin *lovely*, William McFee *harbors of memory*, and Elias Lieberman the one-word refrain from Edgar Allan Poe's "The Raven"—*nevermore*.

I can't resist adding my personal choices for the most luminous lines in English poetry. Try reading them aloud and listening to their magic:

> Brightness falls from the air;
> Queens have died young and fair;
> Dust hath closed Helen's eye.
>
> —THOMAS NASH

Nevermore!

In Xanadu did Kubla Khan
A stately pleasure dome decree
—Samuel Taylor Coleridge

She walks in beauty, like the night,
Of cloudless climes and starry skies
—Lord Byron

Charmed magic casements, opening on the foam
Of perilous seas, in faery lands forlorn
—John Keats

The moan of doves in immemorial elms,
And murmuring of innumerable bees.
—Alfred, Lord Tennyson

Now that you have read several dozen words that are considered to be the most beautiful in our language, I wonder if you might answer a question. Is it possible that we find these words to be lovely just as much for their meanings and associations as for their sounds? Note, for example, that Dr. Funk's list is filled with birds and flowers. Is *bobolink* really any more attractive a word than *condor*, aside from its associations? Is *oriole* really more beautiful than *starling*, or, for that matter, are *thrush* and *hush* any more euphonious than *mush* and *crush*?

Elias Lieberman may find *nevermore* gorgeous to the ear, but H. L. Mencken once quoted a Chinese boy who was learning the English language as saying that *cellar door* was the most musical combination of sounds he had ever heard. One also thinks of the Mexican poet who picked out *cuspidor* as the most beautiful word in English.

Clearly the impact that words have upon us is baffling. Sound and meaning work their dual magic upon us in ways that ear and mind alone cannot always analyze. Consider, for example, the foreign couple who decided to name their first daughter with the most beautiful English word they had ever heard.

They named the child Diarrhea.

Alliteration Strikes the Nation

I am an alliteration addict, a slave to the seductions of sequential syllables starting with the same sound.

Even as a baby I alliterated before I could speak a sentence. "Da-da," "ma-ma," and "bye-bye," I would gurgle gleefully. When I got a little older, I read stories and rhymes about Jack and Jill, Simple Simon, Miss Muffet, King Cole, Boy Blue, Red Riding Hood, Peter Peter Pumpkin Eater, Georgie Porgie Pudding and Pie, and Jack the Giant Killer ("fee fie foe fum . . ."), while in my comic books I followed the amusing adventures of Bugs Bunny, Porky Pig, Little Lulu, Wee Willie Winkle, Beetle Bailey, Hagar the Horrible, Donald and Daffy Duck, and Mickey, Minnie, and Mighty Mouse.

Feeding on french fries and chomping on chocolate chip cookies, munching on marshmallows and quaffing

Coca-Cola, I sat watching "Romper Room," "Sesame Street," and "Captain Kangaroo" while commercials told me that M&M's melt in my mouth and that I'd better buy Birdseye and go for the gusto with a Ford in my future. Out on the street I played Kick the Can, Ring around the Rosy, and Simon Says, all the while chanting, "Eenie meenie minie moe," "Peter Piper picked a peck of pickled peppers," "How much wood would a woodchuck chuck?", and "Sticks and stones may break my bones, but names will never hurt me."

As I grew older, I picked up other words to the wise, like "Practice makes perfect," "A miss is as good as a mile," "Look before you leap," "Where there's a will, there's a way," and "Curiosity killed the cat." And when the fickle finger of fate pointed me down the primrose path to great literature, I ravenously read everything from *Charlie and the Chocolate Factory* to *The Wind in the Willows*, *Piers Plowman* to *Pride and Prejudice*, and *Sir Gawaine and the Green Knight* to *The Great Gatsby*.

Leapin' lizards and jumpin' Jehosephat! You can bet your bottom dollar that I am an alliteration addict—a shell-shocked sad sack beating his breast and caught betwixt and between the devil and the deep blue sea, leaping from the frying pan into the fire on the road to rack and ruin. In wending my way through the whys and wherefores of this alluring activity, I shall not shilly shally, dilly dally, hem and haw, beat around the bush, wear out my welcome, pull any punches, leave you in the lurch, make a mountain out of a molehill, or throw the baby out with the bathwater. After all, I'm not a prim-and-proper, dry-as-dust, dull-as-dishwater, down-in-the-dumps worrywart; a lily-livered, knock-kneed, mild-mannered, mealy-mouthed, daydream-

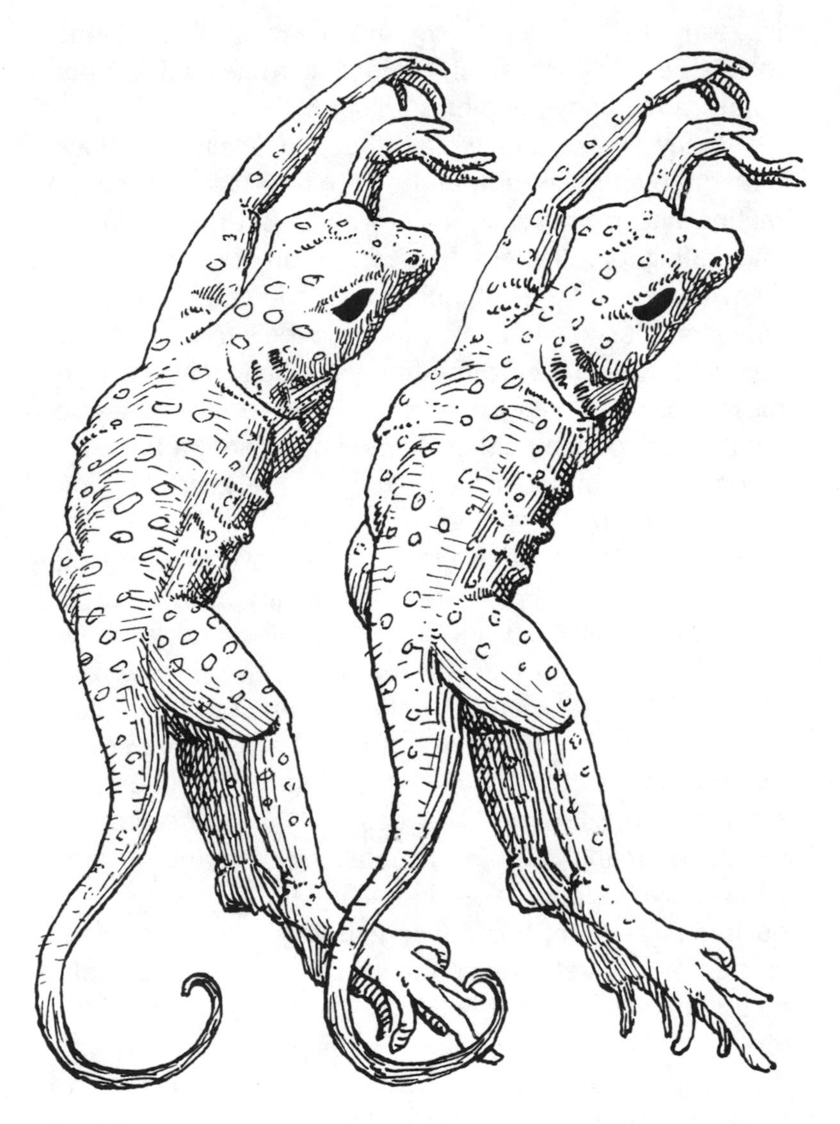

Leapin' lizards!

ing, tongue-tied, wishy-washy nice nelly; or a backbiting, too-big-for-his-britches, birdbrained, hard-headed, bottom-of-the-barrel, party-pooping spoilsport.

Pretty please, don't raise the roof, clean my clock, throw a temper tantrum, and take me to task for being a ranting and raving crazy coot with bats in my belfry; a tattle-taling four-flusher who's out to run you ragged from stem to stern and pillar to post; or a hard-hearted, bamboozling, four-flushing flimflam man who feels free to get your goat and, to add fuel to the fire and insult to injury, or to make a monkey out of you with farfetched tales of fiddle-faddle that contain neither rhyme nor reason, a bunch of baloney that you need like a hole in the head. My conscience is clear.

Good grief! Mind your manners, have a heart, and hold your horses. I may be fat and forty and worse for wear, but, to tell the truth, turn the tables, and lay down the law, I prefer to take the proof positive off the back burner, put the fat on the fire, bring home the bacon, and talk turkey; to come clean and bite the bullet—first and foremost and sure as shootin'—by taking a no-nonsense, down-and-dirty, daredevil, death-defying, rip-roaring, rough-and-ready, fast-and-furious, mile-a-minute, wild-and-woolly, bolt-from-the-blue approach in beating the bushes to pinpoint this hale-and-hearty, short-and-sweet, spic-and-span, safe-and-sound, shipshape, fit-as-a-fiddle, picture-perfect, worthwhile, calm, cool, and collected tip-top topic.

In fact, throughout this entire chapter I've tried to prime the pump, come hell or high water; to bend over backward to practice what I preach; to show the method in my madness (and the madness in my method) with wit and wisdom; to give it a go with get up and go; to show the courage of my convictions with vim and vigor and derring-do; to shape up or ship out by going great guns to beat the band; to leave you pleased as punch and jumping for joy head over heels; and to lay it on the line, bag and baggage, part and parcel, and kit and caboodle to convince you that there's more here than meets the eye.

Last but not least, before I call it quits, head for the hills, burn my bridges behind me, and bid you a fond farewell, I hope you've wholeheartedly enjoyed this treasure trove of tried and true, bright-eyed and bushy-tailed, bread-and-butter, bigger-and-better, larger-than-life, cream-of-the-crop, clear-cut (not haphazard, halfhearted, or mickey mouse) alliterative expressions (the more the merrier), all of them good as gold, worth a pretty penny, a chunk of change, and big bucks, hardly a dime a dozen. Dollars to doughnuts, that's what happens when you go from rags to riches and put your money where your mouth is.

Rhyme Time

Like alliteration, we usually think of rhyme as a musical device found only in poems or commercials: "Flick your Bic," "More bounce to the ounce." But, in fact, rhyme appeals so powerfully to the human ear that, if we listen carefully, we can discover a surprising number of common everyday words and phrases that contain rhyme. Let's sneak a peek at the saga of Chicken Licken:

Once upon a rhyme time, true blue Chicken Licken got the heebie-jeebies that the sky was falling. Dashing pell-mell, helter-skelter, higgledy-piggledy, hither and thither, here, there, and everywhere, and shouting, "Yoo-hoo. May Day! May Day!", Chicken Licken came upon Henny Penny, a roly-poly, jelly-bellied old hen no longer in her heyday. Sensible as she was, Henny Penny huffed and puffed at Licken, "Tee-hee. I don't want to create ill will,

"The sky is falling!"

but what's all this hustle bustle, hubbub, and hurly-burly about? Your tale sounds like a lot of phoney baloney, folderol, razzamatazz, claptrap, and mumbo jumbo to me. I don't believe in abracadabra and hocus-pocus voodoo, and I don't want to kowtow to a hodgepodge of pie in the sky. After all, haste makes waste."

"Jeepers creepers and holy moley, that's a low blow," maintained Licken, whose spirits now flew at half-staff and who was feeling left high and dry. "You forget that a stitch in time saves nine. It's no picnic trying to do my fair share by being fair and square to all those near and dear to me, and you're making such a to-do by taking potshots and calling my story a rinky-dinky hunk of junk. Well, I'm no Humpty-Dumpty crumbum, and your opinion isn't what will make or break me. I may cry, 'boo hoo,' but I'm not going to become a panhandling, rumdum hobo or commit harikari."

Backtracking, Licken ran off looking for Cocky Locky to tell him that the sky was falling. But Locky was too busy being a super-duper hotshot smoking Old Golds and Pall Malls and a hoity-toity wheeler-dealer who each day would ride downtown on the bar car and each week would pay his way on night flights with expensive air fares to wine and dine with fancy-schmancy, polo-playing bigwigs and jet-set fat cats trading on walkie-talkies for big paydays, the name of the game.

Feeling the wear and tear of walking a fine line through a stress test, off Licken scurried to Goosey Loosey, who was indeed loose as a goose and snug as a bug in a rug. "Hey, you old son of a gun," honked Goosey. "Don't be a wishy-washy namby-pamby. Let's go with the flow. I've got a crackerjack, killer-diller, no-fuss-no-muss idea that'll knock your block and socks off. Let's get down to the nitty-gritty and hustle our bustle to a spring fling wingding full of artsy-fartsy Dead Heads feeling their flower power. With the fans wearing backpacks, razzle-dazzle tie-dyed shirts, and zoot suits, it'll be a real blast from the past. It'll be better than prime time on the boob tube—a sure cure for all your gloom and doom. We'll hobnob and get palsy walsy with rich bitches with hi-fis and hotsy-totsy tootsie-wootsies who sit in the grandstand and who get sky-high and ready to do handstands on the bandstand. Then these cutesy-wutesy chicks are liable to do the hootchy-kootchy, hokey pokey, boogie-woogie, or a fantan dance and get real lovey dovey and hot to trot, ready to make hanky-panky. We'll be made in the shade and in like Flynn—in seventh heaven with all those freebies, which I promise we'll share even Stephen. But if you want to be a fuddy-duddy no-show, then it's see you later, alligator. As I always say, different strokes for different folks."

"After a while, crocodile, but not while the sky is falling," said Licken, and he ran to waylay his friend Turkey Lurkey. But plug-ugly Lurkey wasn't any help either. In fact, the redhead was more harum-scarum flibberty gibberty than Licken, acting like a Silly Billy bozo, a run-and-gun local-yokel hillbilly pogo sticking around willy-nilly and hugger mugger like a herky-jerky nitwit, a lamebrain who was drunk as a skunk with a peg leg. "What can one itsy-bitsy, teeny-weeny sky falling down matter?" gobbled Lurkey like a ding-a-ling kiwi trying to play an oboe and hurdy-gurdy at the same time.

Feeling like a Hottentot with ants in his pants, Chicken Licken decided that his court of last resort was to get back on track by consulting Foxy Loxy. Licken was sick of the humdrum responses of the ragtag hoi polloi and their honky-tonk ways, while Loxy's claim to fame was that he was a kind of guru.

"Okeydokey, Licken. Let's have a chalk talk. Your rock 'em-sock 'em story takes the cake and fills the bill, lock, stock, and barrel," said Loxy, with a tutti-frutti smile. "Yo, bro. Let's go to my den for a powwow." So off Licken and Loxy ran to Loxy's cave, where Loxy took out his handy-dandy cookbook and began to speed-read the section on slicing and dicing sweetmeat and Tex-Mex green beans and washing them down with mai tais and Tia Marias. At this Licken sensed a double-trouble melee and yelled, "Ah ha! Oh ho! Who says that might makes right, Einstein? Never ever! Now it's no go, Loxy!"

"Geez Louise and hell's bells, peewee. No pain, no gain," snarled Loxy, looking less and less like a fuzzy-wuzzy Care Bear and more and more lean and mean.

"No way, José," shot back Licken, and he beat it lickety-split before his ass was grass. "This cave needs a sump pump and a pooper scooper, you unsanitary bowwow. I'm off to Fiji, Hong Kong, Malay, Togo, or Zululand—anyplace but here!"

Then wham-bam, thank you, ma'am, the sky fell down and killed them all. And that's what we mean by end rhyme.

VI

English at Play

"Words, words, words."

—WILLIAM SHAKESPEARE

The Play of Words

Welcome to a playground of English words. Step right through the gate and watch some of our strangest and most whimsical words as they clamber over jungle gyms, bounce up and down on seesaws, swing on rings, careen down sliding boards, and merrily whirl around on merry-go rounds.

Most consecutive vowels. Words like *aqueous* and *sequoia* contain four consecutive vowels. *Queueing* contains five in a row, and the word *queue* has the distinction of being the only English word that retains its original pronunciation even when the last four letters are dropped. One word strings together all five major vowels: *miaoued*.

Vowels in order. At least five English words contain the five major vowels in order: *abstemious, abstentious, adventitious, facetious,* and *parecious*. At least six contain

FACETIOUS

the five vowels in reverse order: *duoliteral, quodliteral, subcontinental, uncomplimentary, unoriental,* and *unnoticeably*.

Most letters with one vowel. The longest common word in English that contains but a single vowel is the nine-letter word *strengths*.

Repeated vowels. The longest common English words that contain one repeated vowel, and no other vowel, are *defenselessness* (fifteen letters, five *e*'s) and *strengthlessness* (sixteen letters, four *e*'s). The longest such state names are *Tennessee* (nine letters, four *e*'s) and *Mississippi* (eleven letters, four *i*'s). The sixteen-letter word *indivisibilities* contains seven *i*'s and one *e*.

Most consecutive consonants. Six consonants in a row crowd into the word *latchstring*.

Most letters with one consonant. Several five-letter words tie for the title. *Eerie* is the best example.

Alphabet words. The words *overstuffed* and *understudy* contain four consecutive letters of the alphabet—*rstu*—in order.

Most consecutive letter pairs. The best known example of a word containing three double letters in a row is *bookkeeper*. Perhaps a person who works for a bookkeeper should be called a subbookkeeper.

Most consecutive dots. *Beijing, Fiji,* and *hijinks* (a variant spelling of *high jinks* in some dictionaries) each contain three consecutive dotted letters.

Letter words. A number of words, when pronounced, consist entirely of letter sounds—*essay* (SA), *enemy* (NME), *excellency* (XLNC). The longest such letter string is *expediency* (XPDNC).

Longest palindromic words. A palindrome is a

word, sentence, or longer statement that is spelled the same when its letters are read in reverse order, as those who read on will see. The longest palindromic word entered in English dictionaries is *redivider* (nine letters), although some chemistry handbooks include the eleven-letter palindrome *detartrated.* The longest palindromic cluster embedded in an English word is composed of the first eleven letters in *sensuousness*.

Bilingual reversal. Back in March, 1866, there appeared in *Our Young Folks* magazine an extraordinary English-Latin pairing that reads forward in English and backward in Latin, retaining the same meaning in both languages and both directions:

Anger? 'Tis safe never. Bar it! Use love!
Evoles ut ira breve nefas sit; regna.

Binades. In a binade, a longer word is divided into two shorter words by taking alternate letters in order. Examples include *lounge*: *lug* (odd letters) and *one* (even letters) and *schooled: shoe* (odd letters) and *cold* (even letters).

Snowball words. Snowball words gain bulk as they roll along, one letter at a time. A three-layer snowball word is *damage*: *d am age*. A four-layer example is *fatherless*: *f at her less*. A crystalline five-layer snowballer is *temperamentally*: *t em per amen tally*.

Pyramid words. Words that contain one use of one letter, two uses of a second letter, and so on are called pyramid words. Two examples from our everyday vocabulary are *Tennessee's* (one *t*, two *n*'s, three *s*'s, and four *e*'s) and *sleeveless* (one *v*, two *l*'s, three *s*'s, and four *e*'s).

Longest isograms. An isogram is a word in which no letter of the alphabet appears more than once. The longest English isograms are *ambidextrously* (fourteen letters), *dermatoglyphics* (the science of fingerprints, fifteen letters), and *uncopyrightable* (fifteen letters).

Pair isograms. Some words consist entirely of pairs of letters, each pair occurring once. Among the best examples are *teammate* (eight letters, four pairs), *intestines* (ten letters, five pairs), and *shanghaiings* (twelve letters, six pairs).

Most meanings. The hardest-working word in English is *set*, which in some unabridged dictionaries has almost two hundred meanings. *Run* usually runs a fairly close second.

Most difficult tongue twister. Many people consider *the sixth sick sheikh's sixth sheep's sick* to be the most serpentine tongue twister in English.

Typewriter words. When we seek to find the longest English word that can be written on a single horizontal row of a standard typewriter keyboard, we naturally place our fingers on the top row of letters—*qwertyuiop*—because five of the seven vowels repose there. From that row we can type three ten-letter words: *proprietor*, *perpetuity*, and, with delightful appropriateness, *typewriter*.

Shortest pangrams. Many typists know *The quick brown fox jumps over a lazy dog* as a thirty-three letter sentence that employs every letter in the alphabet at least once. Such sentences are called pangrams. Here is a sampling of the best pangrams of even fewer letters:

- *Pack my box with five dozen liquor jugs.* (thirty-two letters)

- *Jackdaws love my big sphinx of quartz.* (thirty-one)
- *How quickly daft jumping zebras vex.* (thirty)
- *Quick wafting zephyrs vex bold Jim.* (twenty-nine)
- *Waltz, nymph, for quick jigs vex Bud.* (twenty-eight)
- *Bawds jog, flick quartz, vex nymphs.* (twenty-seven)
- *Mr. Jock, TV quiz Ph.D., bags few lynx.* (twenty-six)

If you can come up with a twenty-six letter pangram that makes easy sense and does not resort to names or initials, rush it to me and I'll make you famous.

Anagrammatical English

Can you create one word out of the letters in *new door*? The answer (ha, ha) is *one word.*

An anagram is the rearrangement of the letters in a word or phrase. For more than twenty centuries lovers of word play have found a challenging and amusing exercise of the mind in changing around the letters of anagrammatical words.

Let's start with the points of the compass—*north, south, east,* and *west*. By reshuffling all the letters in each of the four words, what new words can you create? Answers: *north* yields *thorn*; *south* contains *shout*; *east* sparks forth *seat*, *sate*, *eats*, and *teas*; and *west* gives us *stew* and *wets*.

Some words are so kaleidoscopic that they turn out to be perfect anagrams, rearranging themselves to form at least as many words as there are letters in the original word. There are many three-letter examples of perfect anagrams, such as *won, now, own* and *pat, tap, apt*. In the word *eat* we have a looping anagram: Move the first letter to the back and the past tense of the verb, *ate*, emerges; move the first letter to the back again and form the beverage we often drink after we eat, *tea*. Four-letter examples of perfect anagrams include *team*, *tame*, *meat*, *mate; name, mane, mean, amen; time, item, mite, emit; star, tsar, arts, rats, tars.* Have you ever noticed that the STOP you see on a stop sign yields six different four-letter words? The following little poem shows how:

> Our landlord *opts* to fill our *pots*
> Until the *tops* flow over.
> Tonight we *stop* upon this *spot*,
> Tomorrow *post* for Dover.

Perfect five-letter anagram strings exist, like *lapse, pleas, leaps, pales,* and *sepal,* as do strings of seven different words: *spare, pears, pares, spear, reaps, rapes,* and *parse*.

The joys of anagramming that most *aspire* to *praise* are found in changing a word or phrase into another word or phrase that is strikingly appropriate, as in the stunning insights that *eleven plus two* is the same as *twelve plus one*, that when we are *angered,* we are *enraged,* that when we are *wired,* we are *weird,* and that *astronomers* are *moon starers* who would be saddened if there were *no more stars.*

The *evil* thoughts that *live* in us are *vile* and may cast a *veil* over us. Even *Santa* can turn into *Satan* and the

Santa/Satan

United Nations into *tainted unions,* and the *sainted* become *stained instead.* Even your *teachers* can turn into *cheaters* and your *mentors* become a *monster*. It doesn't take much for a *marital* life to become a *martial* life, even in the case of a *married admirer*. Then that which was *sacred* may make you *scared*, and that which was *united* may become *untied*.

Am I getting *groans* from your *organs* with all this word play so that with *determination* you exclaim, *"I mean to rend it!"*? Good, do not remain *silent*. I *enlist* you to *listen* to an even more ingenious kind of anagram. Now the word or phrase brings forth a second word or phrase that is surprisingly apt:

Gold and silver are often *grand old evils*. They may lead to *degradedness*, which is *greed's sad end*, or to *villainousness*, *an evil soul's sin*. Then comes a *penitentiary*: *nay, I repent it; punishment: nine thumps; a sentence of death* that *faces one at the end;* and finally *desperation: a rope ends it*.

Isn't it sad that *a shoplifter* always *has to pilfer*; that *prosecutors* are often *court posers* in whose *conversation* often *voices rant on*; that a *misanthrope* is likely to say about a beggar, "*Spare him not*"; and that *medical consultations* occasionally turn out to be *noted miscalculations*?

In *the nudist colony* we find *no untidy clothes*, just as in *the countryside* we find *no city dust here*. A *problem in Chinese* is usually *incomprehensible*. One blessed with *softheartedness often sheds tears* and utters *endearments: tender names*. *Metaphysicians* are *mystics in a heap* and *a spellbinder* is a *bland spieler*. *Upholsterers* try to *restore plush*, and a *waitress* may be heard to ask, *"A stew, sir?"* The *telegraph* is certainly a *great help*. And in the spirit of patriotism we may say of *the United States of America* that it *attaineth its cause—freedom!*

Turning to religion, we discover that the *serpent* in the Garden of Eden *repents* at *present*; that despite Nebuchadnezzar's *denial, Daniel nailed* and *alined* him with a curse; that one who practices *Christianity* might exclaim, *"I cry that I sin!"*; and that in its beginnings a *monastery* tolerated *no mastery* from *nasty Rome*, truly an *amen story* (as well as a quadruple anagram). One of the oldest and best-known anagrams is fashioned from a question that Pilate asked of Jesus: *Quid est veritas?* (What is truth?) The answer was already contained in the question: *Est vir adest.* (It is the man who is here.)

No wonder that those of us who believe in the magical potency of words have hailed *anagrams* as *ars magna*, the "great art."

Doctor Rotcod's Ailihphilia

Some people are destined for greatness, others for mediocrity. Otto Rotcod was born to become the palindrome made flesh. The date of Rotcod's nativity was September 3, 1939—9/3/39, an arrangement of figures that reads the same left to right and right to left—in Danbury, New Hampshire, the only area of the state with a self-reflecting ZIP code—03230. His palindromic dad, Bob, and palindromic mom, Ava, named their tot Otto.

When Rotcod was a student in junior high school, he wrote a history paper on the career of George W. Goethals, the American engineer who masterminded the building of the Panama Canal. At the end of his report, young Otto summarized Goethals's achievement by writing: "*A man! A plan! A canal! Panama!*" Rotcod surveyed his sentence with considerable pride and discovered that the statement

Doctor Otto Rotcod

was a palindrome, causing him to exclaim: *"A man! A plan! A canal! Panama!" sides reversed is "A man! A plan! A canal! Panama!"* On a hunch, Rotcod wrote down that exclamation and saw that it too was palindromic, yielding a mirror image of itself.

At that epiphanous moment of fearful symmetry, Rotcod became a lifelong cainamaniac—a ciloholic who spoke and wrote only in palindromes. *Ah ha!* he yelled. Years later, Rotcod became a doctor to realize the unfulfilled potential of his surname. Naturally, he married a woman named Hannah, and from their union issued five well-balanced daughters—Ada, Anna, Eve, Lil, and Nan. Having heard about this strange case of linguistic behavior, I recently visited the good doctor in his New Hampshire office and conducted an interview:

LEDERER: Dr. Rotcod, I'll begin by asking you about your preferences in life. Whom do you prefer, your father, Bob, or your mother, Ava?

—ROTCOD: *Pa's a sap.*

So you like your mother better?

—*Ma is as selfless as I am.*

What about your choice between Coke and Pepsi?

—*Pepsi is pep.*

Between Japanese and American cars?

—*Race car?*

No, sedan.

—*A Toyota.*

And your second choice?

—*Civic.*

Is golf your favorite sport?

—*Golf? No sir! Prefer prison-flog.*

Which do you like better, mathematics or science?

—*I prefer pi.*

Odd or even numbers?

—*Never odd or even.*

Would you rather go to a movie or stay at home and watch television?

—*Same nice cinemas.*

I'd like to explore your political preferences. What do you do each presidential election?

—*Rise to vote, sir.*

And who do you feel has been our greatest president?

—*Name now one man.*

All right. Franklin D. Roosevelt.

—*Tut-tut. Star comedy by Democrats. Tut-tut.*

Then you are a Republican?

—*Hey, yeh.*

Let's move on to your career in medicine. What would you do first for a student who came to you with inflamed gums?

—*Draw pupil's lip upward.*

And what tranquilizer would you recommend?

—*Xanax.*

What do you tell patients who are sexually worn out?

—*Sex at noon taxes.*

Is it true that you apply straw to warts?

—*Straw? No. Too stupid a fad. I put soot on warts.*

I understand that you were recently visited by a hermit with stomach problems.

—*Recluse's ulcer?*

Yes, what kind of diet did you recommend?

—*Stressed desserts.*

You emphasized desserts in that diet?

—*I saw desserts; I'd no lemons, alas, no melon; distressed was I.*

And is it true that you encouraged the patient to consume alcoholic beverages?

—*Yo! Bottoms up—U. S. motto. Boy!*

Did you recommend lager or red rum?

—*Peels's lager. Red rum did murder regal sleep.*

I understand that, when none of these ideas worked, you recommended that the patient try losing weight by fasting. What did he say?

—*"Doc, note, I dissent. A fast never prevents a fatness. I diet on cod."*

Doctor Rotcod, in addition to your fame in medical circles, you are well known for your passionate hatred of evil.

—*Evil is name of a foeman, as I live.*

Then what is your advice to those who seek the good life?

—*Live not on evil.*

How can one do that?

—*Repel evil as a live leper.*

Do you then wish to stamp out all lies?

—*Live on evasions? No! I save no evil.*

How should one treat a liar?

—*Rail at a liar.*

Can good and evil exist together in this world?

—*No, it is in opposition.*

Did evil always exist?

—*O, stone me! Not so!*

Then where did evil begin?

—*Eve.*

"Madam in Eden, I'm Adam."

And Adam, too?

—*Mad Adam.*

What did Adam say when he first met Eve?

—*Madam in Eden, I'm Adam.*

And what did Eve say?

—*Eve, maiden name. Both sad in Eden? I dash to be manned. I am Eve.*

What happened when Eve saw that jewel of a forbidden fruit?

—*Eve saw diamond, erred. No maid was Eve.*

And what happened when Eve offered the fruit to Adam?

—*Won't lovers revolt now?*

So they sinned together?

—*Named under a ban—a bared nude man.*

And the result was . . . ?

—*Eve damned Eden, mad Eve.*

Can we ever escape the influence of that act?

—*Her Eve's noose we soon sever, eh?*

Well, can we?

—*No, evils live on.*

Were you ever so innocent that you did not know sin?

—*Snug, raw was I ere I saw war guns.*

And when you grew older, did you ever sin, Doctor?

—*Lived as a devil.*

How so?

—*Evil did I dwell; lewd did I live.*

And what was the result of that life?

—*Reviled did I live; evil I did deliver.*

Apparently, you began to despair of ever overcoming evil. What were you thinking?

—*Do good's deeds live on? No, evil's deeds do, O God.*

I imagine that this state of affairs made you quite miserable.

—*Egad, a base life defiles a bad age.*

Did you ever despair that evil could be conquered?

—*No, it can—action!*

So you dedicated your life to fighting evil?

—*Now do I repay a period won.*

And you fought evil with good?

—*Did I do, O God, did I as I said I'd do? Good, I did!*

Have you finally won your battle against sin?

—*Now, sir, a war is won.*

Do you feel good about all this?

—*Revered now I live on. O did I do no evil, I wonder, ever?*

I understand that your colleagues in virtue have no doubts that they will have their reward in heaven.

—*Nor I, fool. Ah, no! We won halo—of iron!*

And what will happen to you few who have seen the light?

—*Are we not drawn onward, we few, drawn onward to new era?*

Doctor Rotcod, I thank you for this scintillating two-way interview. But how do you do it? How are you able to speak in palindromes so skillfully?

—*Because if I didn't, I'd sound something like this: "sihte kilg niht emos dnuos ditn didifie suaceb."*

VII

The Last Word About Words

"Stability in language is synonymous with rigor mortis."

—Ernest Weekley

The Antics of Semantics

Has it ever struck you how human words are? Like people, words are born, grow up, get married, have children, and even die. They may be very old, like *man* and *wife* and *grass* and *home*; they may be very young, like *moonwalk*, *break dancing*, *househusband*, and *veggies*. They may be newly born and struggling to live, as *televangelist*, *veejay*, *sound bite*, and *computer virus*; or they may repose in the tomb of history, as *leechcraft*, the Anglo-Saxon word for the practice of medicine, and *murfles*, a long defunct word for freckles or pimples.

Our lives are filled with people and words, and in both cases we are bound to be impressed with their vast numbers and infinite variety. Some words, like *OK*, are famous all over the world; others, like *foozle* (a bungling golf stroke) and *groak* (to stare at other people's food, hoping that they will offer you some) are scarcely known, even at home. There are some words that we will probably never meet, such as *schizocarps* (the pinwheels that grow on maple trees) and *vomer* (the slender bone separating the nostrils), and others that are with us practically every day of our lives, such as *I*, *the*, *and*, *to*, and *of*, the five most frequently used English words.

As with people, words have all sorts of shapes, sizes, backgrounds, and personalities. They may be very large, like *pneumonoultramicroscopicsilicovolcanoconiosis*, a forty-five-letter hippopotomonstrosesquipedalian word for a lung congestion contracted by language book writers who poke their noses into too many old, dusty dictionaries. They may be very small, like *a* and *I*.

Some words are multinational in their heritage, as *remacadamize*, which is Latin, Celtic, Hebrew, and Greek in parentage; some come of old English stock, as *sun* and *moon* and *grass* and *goodness*; some have a distinctly continental flavor—*kindergarten, lingerie, spaghetti;* others are unmistakably American—*stunt* and *baseball*.

Words like *remunerative*, *encomium*, and *perspicacious* are so dignified that they can intimidate us, while others, like *booze*, *burp*, and *blubber*, are markedly undignified in character. Some words, such as *ecdysiast*, H. L. Mencken's Greek-derived name for a stripteaser, love to put on fancy airs; others, like *vidiot* and *palimony*, are winkingly playful. Certain words strike us as rather beautiful, like *luminous* and *gossamer*, others as rather ugly—*guzzle* and *scrod*; some as quiet—*dawn* and *dusk*; others as noisy—*thunder* and *crash*.

Many words evolve over the centuries and reflect the sometimes slow, sometimes instant changes in human

A muskrat living in France . . .

society. A muskrat living in France is pretty much the same as one living in England, just as a twentieth-century muskrat behaves in much the same manner as its sixteenth-century ancestors. But a human being living in America today is vastly different from a person who lived during the European Renaissance. So it is with words: what they once meant is not necessarily what they mean now. Words have life after birth. Words wander wondrously.

As one example of how the meaning of a word can change very quickly, have a look at a passage from *The Octopus*, written by the American novelist Frank Norris in 1901:

> Lyman Derrick sat dictating letters to his typewriter . . .
>
> "That's all for the present," he said at length.
>
> Without reply, the typewriter rose and withdrew, thrusting her pencil into the coil of her hair, closing the door behind her, softly, discreetly. (*Book II, Chapter I*)

Norris was not fabricating a science-fiction tale featuring robot typewriters. Rather, in his day a typewriter was a person who worked on a typewriting machine, not the machine itself.

Any reader of the works of William Shakespeare knows the wayward ways that words wend over the centuries. Take *Hamlet*. When the Prince of Denmark, resolving to remember and avenge his father's murder, cries, "Yea from the table of my memory/I'll wipe away all trivial fond records," he is using *table* in its earlier sense of "a tablet" and *fond* in its earlier meaning of "foolish." When the

Melancholy Dane laments, "Things rank and gross in nature possess it merely," he is using *merely* to mean "absolutely, entirely," just the opposite of today's denotation.

When Hamlet goes to see his mother in her closet, he does not visit her in a tiny room where her clothes are stored. To Shakespeare and his contemporaries, a closet was a bedchamber. In this scene, Hamlet shows the Queen two portraits, "the counterfeit presentment of two brothers." Pointing to the picture of Claudius, Hamlet cries, "Here is your husband, like a mildewed ear,/Blasting his wholesome brother."

Queen Gertrude then sobs, "Thou turn'st my eyes into my very soul,/And there I see such black and grained spots/As will not leave their tinct." In this exchange, *counterfeit* signifies "likeness," *blasting* "poisoning," *wholesome* "healthy," *leave* "lose," and *tinct* "color."

One reason for the various revisions of the King James version of the Bible is that many of the words as they existed in the early seventeenth century are no longer in use or no longer have the same meaning. In the King James Bible, *wealth* means "well being," *allege* means "to prove," *comprehend* "to overcome," *demand* "to ask," and *take no thought* means "be not anxious."

In Genesis, we read: "And Joseph made haste; for his bowels did yearn upon his brother." Obviously *bowels* possessed a different meaning in Middle and early Modern English—"the center of the emotions." Most modern readers are puzzled by the word *naughty* as it appears in this passage in the Book of Jeremiah: "One basket had very good figs, even like the figs that are first ripe: and the other basket had very naughty figs, which could not be eaten, they were so bad." The puzzle is solved when we learn that *naught* and *nought* were once simply variant spellings, and *naught* meant "nought-y, or worthless."

Turning to the New Testament, we note that the Holy Ghost is not a ghost in modern terms but, rather, the Holy Spirit. And, because it has taken on new associations, the word *charity* has been changed to *love* in newer translations of Paul's ringing statement in First Corinthians: "And now abideth faith, hope, charity, these three: but the greatest of these is charity."

The archaic, inconstant meanings of words become vivid and dramatic when we see them in the contexts of long-ago literary passages:

brat: children. "O Israel, O household of the Lord,/O Abraham's brats, O brood of blessed seed."—George Gascoigne, *A Hundred Sundry Flowers*

buxom: yielding. "And buxom to the law."—Langland, *Piers Plowman*

clown: peasant; *corn:* wheat. "The voice I hear this passing night was heard/In ancient days by emperor and clown;/Perhaps the selfsame song that found a path/Through the sad heart of Ruth, when sick for home,/She stood in tears amid the alien corn."—John Keats, "Ode to a Nightingale"

family: household. "I was a single man . . . but I had a family of servants."—Daniel Defoe, *Journal of the Plague Year*

jaunty: noble. "See how finely bred he is, how jaunty and complaisant."—John Crowne, *The Country Wit*

rude: simple. "Each in his narrow cell forever laid/"The rude forefathers of the hamlet sleep."—Thomas Gray, "Elegy Written in a Country Churchyard"

silly: empty, useless. "The silly buckets on the deck/

That had so long remained,/I dreamt that they were filled with dew;/And when I awoke it rained."—Samuel Taylor Coleridge, "Rime of the Ancient Mariner"

Like people, words grow after they are born; once created, they seldom sit still and remain the same forever. Some words expand to take over larger territories. They begin with a precise meaning, but their boundaries widen and often grow fuzzier and less definite. A fabulous example of this expansive process is the word *fabulous*. Once *fabulous* meant "resembling or based on a fable." Later came the meaning "incredible, marvelous" because fables often contained incredible and marvelous characters and events. Nowadays the word is weakening in meaning still more, and anything can be fabulous: The latest styles of blue jeans are fabulous, as is *Paradise Lost*; the latest breakthroughs in computers are fabulous, and so is the current Picasso exhibit. A *picture* was once a painted representation of something seen; now any visual representation—photograph, pen and ink, crayon—is a picture. A *holiday* first signified "a holy day," but modern holidays include secular days off like Valentine's Day and Independence Day. Not only has the *holy* part of the compound generalized, but so has the *day* part. Thus, a holiday can now last more than twenty-four hours, as in the rather British "I'm going on holiday to the Caribbean."

Other words travel in exactly the opposite direction and narrow to acquire more specific meanings than the ones with which they started life. Once at the end of a Chinese meal, my young daughter opened a fortune cookie and read the message inside: "You are genial, clever, intellectual, and discriminating." "But," she protested, "I don't discriminate!" My perceptive child was being sensitive to the fact that *discriminate* has taken on the specialized meaning of making choices in matters of race. Much the same thing has happened to the words *segregation*, *colored*, *chauvinism*, *comrade*, *fairy*, *queer*, and *gay*. In *Little Women* (1870), Louisa May Alcott wrote without any ambiguity whatsoever, "As Mrs. March would say, what can you do with four gay girls in the house?"

No word is born shrinkproof. The older meaning of *meat* was "food," of *liquor* "drink," and of *corn* "grain." *To starve* did not necessarily mean to lack these items. Early in its life, *starve* meant "to perish." A *hound* was originally "a dog," a *fowl* "a bird," and a *deer* "any small animal," as seen in Shakespeare's *King Lear:* "But mice and rats and such small deer/Have been Tom's food for seven long year." Originally the title *doctor* was given to anyone skilled in a learned profession. An *undertaker* once could undertake to do anything; nowadays undertakers specifically undertake to manage funerals. Incredibly, a *girl* once could be a boy, as during the Middle English period *girl* was a unisex word denoting any child or youth.

Business started out as a general term meaning literally "busy-ness; one's proper concern." After a couple of centuries of life, *business* picked up the narrower meaning of "commercial dealings." In 1925 Calvin Coolidge used the word in both its generalized and specialized senses when he stated, "The chief business of the American people is business." We today can see the word starting to generalize back to its first meaning in phrases like "I don't like this funny business one bit."

Some words are born into low station and come up in the world. With the passing of time, certain positions and ranks have acquired *prestige* (which used to mean "trick-

"You are the homeliest woman I have ever met!"

ery") and *glamor* (which began life as a synonym for "grammar"); with these changes, the words describing them have risen from the humble to the exalted. Such are the histories of *knight*, which once meant "a boy," *lord* (loaf giver), *governor* (steersman), *marshal* (house servant), *squire* (shield bearer), *chamberlain* (room attendant), *constable* (stable attendant), *steward* (sty warden), *minister* (servant), and *pedagogue* (slave). In Geoffrey Chaucer's Middle English, *nice*, derived from the Latin *nescius*, "ignorant," meant "foolish, senseless," and in William Shakespeare's day, *politician* was a sinister word implying scheming, machiavellian trickery. Some would argue that the word really hasn't changed very much.

The reputations of other words slide downhill. Human nature being what it is, we are prone to believe the worst about people, and this cynicism is reflected in the fact that word meanings are much more likely to degrade than to upgrade. An Englishman was served a delicious meal in an American household and, afterward, complimented his hostess with "You are the homeliest woman I have ever met!" This was high praise in British English, in which *homely* means "homelike, good around the home." But because it was perceived that women who stayed home were generally unattractive, the word has taken on negative associations in American English. A similar fate has befallen *spinster*, which, as its roots indicate, meant simply "a woman who spins." The Greeks used *idiōtēs*, from the root *idios*, "private," to designate those who did not hold public office. Because such people possessed no special skill or status, the word gradually fell into disrepute.

Stink and *stench* were formerly neutral in meaning

and referred to any smell, as did *reek*, which once had the innocuous meaning of "to smoke, emanate." Shakespeare wrote his great sonnet sequence just at the time that *reek* was beginning to degrade and exploited the double meaning in his whimsical Sonnet 130:

> My mistress' eyes are nothing like the sun,
> Coral is far more red than her lips' red.
> If snow be white, why then her breasts are dun,
> If hair be wires, black wires grow on her head.
> I have seen roses damasked, red and white,
> But no such roses see I on her cheeks.
> And in some perfume there is more delight
> Than in the breath that from my mistress reeks.

The family resemblances between words and people should come as no surprise. After all, language is not something that cave people discovered in the woods or turned up under a rock. Language is a human invention, and humanness is the invention of language. The birth of language is the dawn of humanity, and each is as old as the other. It is people who make up words and it is people who decide what words shall mean, people, who are as mutable and mercurial as the muskrat is constant. From a creature who is a little lower than the angels and a little above the apes, who embraces tiger and lamb, Apollo and Dionysus, the Oedipus Cycle and the Three Stooges, we can expect nothing less or more than a language in which people drive in a parkway and park in a driveway and play at a recital and recite at a play, a language in which a slim chance and a fat chance are the same but a wise man and a wise guy are opposites. From such a changeful and inconstant being we can expect nothing more or less than an outpouring of words that are brightly rational, wonderfully serviceable, maddeningly random, frenetically creative, and, of course, completely crazy.

The Answers

Confusable English (page 28): 1. d 2. c 3. a 4. a 5. b 6. a 7. d 8. a 9. d 10. b 11. a 12. d 13. b 14. a 15. c 16. d 17 c 18. a 19. c 20. b.

Pseudonyms (page 62): 1. George Orwell 2. Mark Twain 3. Boz 4. Lewis Carroll 5. George Eliot 6. Doctor Seuss 7. O. Henry 8. James Herriot 9. Joseph Conrad 10. Saki

About the Author

Author of the national best sellers *Anguished English* and *Get Thee to a Punnery,* Richard Lederer has spent his career careening through the English language. A teacher for twenty-eight years at St. Paul's School in Concord, New Hampshire, he has earned a Ph.D. in linguistics and published more than a thousand articles and books about language. He is a vice-president of SPELL (Society for the Preservation of English Language and Literature) and has been elected Punster of the year by the International Save the Pun Foundation.

Dr. Lederer's weekly column, "Looking at Language," appears in newspapers and magazines throughout the United States. He is the Grammar Grappler for *Writer's Digest,* a regular contributor to *Writing!* and *Verbatim,* and language commentator on New Hampshire Public Radio.